The Complete Christian
Baby Name Book

The Complete Christian Baby Name Book

Over 4,500 Catholic Names of Saints, Angels & Virtues

Including All Names from the Roman Martyrology

Compiled by Nicole M. McGinnis

iUniverse, Inc.
New York Bloomington Shanghai

The Complete Christian Baby Name Book
Over 4,500 Catholic Names of Saints, Angels & Virtues

iUniverse books may be ordered through booksellers or by contacting:

iUniverse
1663 Liberty Drive
Bloomington, IN 47403
www.iuniverse.com
1-800-Authors (1-800-288-4677)

Because of the dynamic nature of the Internet, any Web addresses or links contained in this book may have changed since publication and may no longer be valid.

The views expressed in this work are solely those of the author and do not necessarily reflect the views of the publisher, and the publisher hereby disclaims any responsibility for them.

ISBN: 978-0-595-50978-2 (pbk)
ISBN: 978-0-595-61718-0 (ebk)

Printed in the United States of America

"Finally, a name is given the person baptized. It should be taken from some person whose eminent sanctity has given him a place in the catalogue of the Saints. The similarity of name will stimulate each one to imitate the virtues and holiness of the Saint, and, moreover, to hope and pray that he who is the model for his imitation will also be his advocate and watch over the safety of his body and soul."

—The Catechism of the Council of Trent

In honor of Our Blessed Mother, thy mantle is our safe harbor.

For my loving husband and children, who are all infinitely cherished,

And to my good friend Janel, who has never

gotten sick of our baby name conversations.

All ye holy angels and saints,

Pray for us!

Contents

The Importance of Giving Children Christian Names

"Wherefore those are to be reproved who search for the names of heathens, especially of those who were the greatest monsters of iniquity, to bestow upon their children. By such conduct they practically prove how little they regard Christian piety when they so fondly cherish the memory of impious men, as to wish to have their profane names continually echo in the ears of the faithful." (*The Catechism of the Council of Trent*, p. 197)

"The name of a saint is given in Baptism in order that the person baptized may imitate his virtues and have him for a protector." (*Baltimore Catechism No. 3*, p. 189)

"The names of *angels* are also given, as well as names referring to mysteries or sacred appellations, events, and doctrines ... The Church *does not approve* of heathen or fantastical names, such as combinations taken from a film or novel, or made up from various words ... Some name their children after pagan gods and goddesses, flowers, places, or some wealthy or prominent relative's surname. We hear of Ceres and Europa as names inflicted on poor little girls, when they could have been named after the angels and saints that behold God face to face! What is the most beautiful flower on earth compared to a Saint of God, who can protect and pray for the child! We hear of little boys named with the surname of some figure prominent in politics or finance, instead of the name of an angel or saint, as the Archangel Michael, this flame of God that thrust the rebel hordes into hell." (*My Catholic Faith*, p. 255)

"A **Christian name** should be given a person in Baptism ... If pastors cannot persuade parents to do this they should add the name of a Saint to the one chosen by the parents and enter both names in the baptismal register." (*Moral Theology*, p. 334)

"From the early ages the Church has required baptismal names which have a Christian significance." (*Is It a Saint's Name?*, p. 3)

"It is sad to behold how many parents overlook the importance and great meaning of this religious tradition. Of all things a person can acquire in this life, his name is the first and closest possession; in a way, it is himself. When Our Lord was to be born, God did not leave the choice of the name to human beings. He Himself chose the Saviour's name and considered it important enough to send an Angel to announce His choice to St. Joseph." (*Religious Customs in the Family*, p. 24)

"Thus it can be seen that the name you give your child can have a deep significance for him all his life. His name should symbolize the characteristics you hope to instill, and should inspire him to live up to the virtuous qualities it implies. The child also should be taught as he grows up to look upon the saint he has been named after as a special friend in heaven. Your infant's patron saint may therefore be his mediator before God." (*The Catholic Marriage Manual*, p. 73)

A Note to Parents

Taken from the Foreward in *Is It a Saint's Name?*
Compiled by Rev. William P. Dunne

"In choosing baptismal names parents should keep in mind the thought that the child will hear these names throughout life. They should be careful to avoid names or combinations which will subject the bearer to ridicule. Light and fancy-sounding names should not be given to boys; nicknames should not be given in Baptism; given names should be balanced with the surname. The length of the given names should have a harmonious relation to one another and to the family name. A rhythm and cadence of sound should be sought."

Introduction

When naming my own children, I searched for books with collections of Christian names. Unfortunately, I only found one small book entitled *Is It a Saint's Name?* by Rev. William P. Dunne. While I am forever indebted to Rev. Dunne for his labor of love, I found that because it was written in the 1940s, the book was aimed at listing names that were popular in that era. I was hoping to create a work that would include all names from the Roman Martyrology, and also the names in Rev. Dunne's work, and therefore be rather timeless in nature to those who might want such an expansive list.

Please understand my desire is to present all possible Christian names for the reader. I certainly do not recommend that all of the names are fit to be given to a child in our present day, but perhaps in a few more decades names that seem outlandish today would be perfectly prudent gifts to our children.

This work has also included all readily available name meanings, their respective countries of origin, and the feast days of each saint. Please note that there are frequently several saints with the same name and usually the first saint listed in the Roman Martyrology is the one used for the feast day. A name in parentheses is the saint's name in which that variation originated from.

I pray that this book will be useful to you. Enjoy!

Boys

A

Aaron: Hebrew "revered; sharer"	July 1
Abachum	Jan. 19
Abban: Irish "little abbot"	Oct. 27
Abdechalas	Apr. 21
Abdias	Nov. 19
Abdiesus	Apr. 22
Abdon: Greek "God's worker"	July 30
Abel: Hebrew "vital; breath"	Dec. 2
Abercius: Latin "open mind"	Oct. 22
Abibo	Aug. 3
Abibus	Nov. 15
Abilius	Feb. 22
Abilias	
Abraham: Hebrew "fathering multitudes"	Oct. 9
Abram: Hebrew "high father"	
Absalon: Hebrew "peaceful; handsome"	Mar. 2
Abudemius	July 15
Abundantius	Mar. 1
Abundius	Feb. 27

Acacius: Latin "blameless"   Mar. 31
    Achates

Acathius   May 8

Acatius   Apr. 9

Accurtius   Jan. 16
    Accursius

Acepsimas   Apr. 22

Achilles: Greek   Nov. 7
    Achille, Achillas

Achilleus   May 12

Achim (Joachim)   Aug. 16

Achmed   Dec. 24

Acindynus   Apr. 20

Acisclus   Nov. 17

Acutius   Sept. 19

Acylinus   July 17
    Acyllinus

Adalbert   Apr. 23

Adam: Hebrew "first man; original; earth"   Dec. 24

Adauctus   Aug. 30

Adaucus: Latin "audacious"   Feb. 7

Adelbert   June 25

Adelf   Aug. 29
    Adelphus

Aderitus   Sept. 27

Adjutor   Sept. 1

Adjutus   Jan. 16

Ado: American "respected"   Dec. 16

Adolph: German "sly wolf" — Sept. 27
    Adolfo: Italian, Spanish, **Adophe, Adolphus**

Adrian: Latin "wealthy; dark-skinned" — Mar. 4
    Adrien

Adrion — May 17
    Adrio

Adulf — Sept. 27

Adventor — Nov. 20

Aedesius — Apr. 8

Aelred — Jan. 12

Aemilian — Feb. 8

Aemilius — May 22

Aeneas (Angus): Greek, Latin "to praise" — Mar. 11

Aetherius — Mar. 4

Africanus — Apr. 10

Agabius — Aug. 4

Agabus — Feb. 13

Agape: Greek "love" — Jan. 25

Agapitus — Mar. 16

Agapius: Greek "love" — Aug. 19

Agathangelus — Jan. 23

Agatho — Jan. 10

Agathodorous — Mar. 4

Agathonicus — Aug. 22

Agathopodes — Apr. 4

Agericus — Dec. 1

Aggaeus — Jan. 4

Agileus — Oct. 15

Aglibert	June 24
Agnellus	Dec. 14
Agoard	June 24
Agricola: Irish "farms"	Mar. 17
Agrippinus	Nov. 9
Agritius	Jan. 13
Aicard **Aichard, Achart**	Sept. 15
Aidan: Irish "fiery spirit" **Aiden**: English	Aug. 31
Aigulphus **Aigulph**	Sept. 3
Ailbe	Sept. 12
Aime: French	Sept. 13
Aithalas	Apr. 22
Aithilahas	Mar. 14
Alain: French "handsome boy"	Oct. 26
Alair (Hilary)	Jan. 14
Alan: Irish "handsome boy"	Oct. 26
Alaric: German "noble ruler"	Sept. 29
Alban: Latin "white man; from Alba's white hill" **Albany**	June 22
Albert: German "distinguished" **Albrecht, Alberto**: Italian, Spanish, **Albertino**	Nov. 15
Albian	June 10
Albin: Scandinavian "white; bright"	Mar. 1
Albinus	Feb. 5
Alcuin	May 19

Aldhelm **Adhelm**	May 25
Alexander: Greek "great leader; helpful" **Alessandro**: Italian, **Alexandre**	Jan. 11
Alexis: English **Alexian, Alexio, Alexios, Aleixo**: Galician, **Alexe, Alessio**: Italian	Feb. 17
Alexius: Greek "helper; defender"	July 17
Alfred: English "counselor"	Aug. 15
Alger: German "hardworking"	Apr. 11
Alipius	Aug. 15
Allan: English "handsome" **Allen**	Jan. 12
Alleyn	Feb. 22
Almachius	Jan. 1
Aloysius: German "famed; famous warrior" **Alois, Aloisio, Aloys**	June 21
Alpheus: Hebrew "follower; successor"	Nov. 17
Alphius	May 10
Alphonsus: Latin "distinguished" **Alfons, Alfonso**: Italian, Spanish "ready for battle", **Alonso, Alphonse**: Spanish "ready for battle", **Alphonso**	Aug. 2
Alpinian	June 30
Alton (Alto): Old English "old town"	Feb. 9
Alvin: Latin "light-haired; loved; elf; supernatural being; friend"	Dec. 7
Amadeo: Italian "blessed by God; artistic"	Apr. 18
Amadeus: Latin "God-loving; God's love"	Jan. 28
Amand	Feb. 6
Amandus	June 18
Amantius	Feb. 10

Amaranthus   Nov. 7

Amarinus   Jan. 25

Amator   Apr. 30

Amatus   Aug. 31

Ambicus   Dec. 3

Ambrose: Greek "everlasting; immortal"   Dec. 7
    Ambrosio, Ambroise, Ambrozi

Americus (Emmeric)   Nov. 4
    Almeric, Americo, Amerigo: Italian "home ruler", **Amery, Amory**:
    Old German "home strength"

Ammian   Sept. 4

Ammon: Irish "hidden", Hebrew "teacher, builder"   Sept. 1

Ammonius   Jan. 18

Amos: Hebrew "strong; to carry; borne by God"   Mar. 31

Ampelius   Feb. 11

Ampelus   Nov. 20

Amphian   Apr. 2

Amphilochius   Mar. 27

Amphion   June 12

Ampliatus   Oct. 31

Anacharius   Sept. 25

Anacletus   July 13

Ananias: "pious"   Jan. 25

Anastasius: Greek "reborn"   Jan. 9

Anathalo   Sept. 24

Anatole: French "exotic", Greek "break of day"   July 3
    Anatol

Anatolius   Mar. 20

Ancel (Lancelot): French "creative"	June 27
Andeol	May 1
Andochius	Sept. 24
Andrew: Greek "manly and brave; warrior" **Anders**: Scandinavian, **Andrea, Andrus, Andres**: Spanish	Jan. 6
Andre: French "masculine"	May 13
Andronicus: Greek "clever"	Oct. 11
Anectus	Mar. 10
Anempodistus	Nov. 2
Anesius	Mar. 31
Angelo: Italian	May 5
Angelus	May 5
Angus: Celtic, Scottish "standout; important; one choice"	Mar. 11
Anian	Apr. 25
Anicetus	Apr. 17
Anno	Dec. 4
Ansanus	Dec. 1
Ansbert	Feb. 8
Anselm: German "protective; God's helmet" **Ansel**: French "follower of a nobleman; creative", **Anselme, Anselmo**	Apr. 21
Ansgar	Feb. 3
Ansovinus	Mar. 13
Anterus	Jan. 3
Anthelmus	June 26
Anthes	Aug. 28
Anthimus	May 11

Anthony: Latin "outstanding"	June 13
Anton, Antoni, Antonie, Antonio	
Antidius	June 17
Antigonus	Feb. 27
Antiochus	May 21
Antinogenes	July 24
Antipas: Greek "father"	Apr. 11
Antonine	Apr. 20
Antoninus	May 10
Antony: Latin "good"	Jan. 17
Anysius	Dec. 30
Apelles	Apr. 22
Apellius	Sept. 10
Aper	Sept. 15
Aphraates	Apr. 7
Aphrodisius	Mar. 14
Aphthonius	Nov. 2
Apian	Apr. 2
Apodemius	Apr. 16
Apollinaris	Jan. 5
Apollo: Greek "masculine; destroyer"	Apr. 21
Apollonius	Apr. 10
Apphias	Nov. 22
Appian	Dec. 30
Apronian	Feb. 2
Apulcius	Oct. 7
Aquilinus	Jan. 4

Aquinas	Mar. 7
Aquin	
Arator	Apr. 21
Arbogastus: "covered"	July 21
Arcadius	Jan. 12
Archelaus: Greek "the people's ruler"	Mar. 4
Archibald: German "bold leader; genuine"	Mar. 27
Archimimus	Mar. 29
Archippus	Mar. 20
Arcontius	Sept. 5
Ardalion	Apr. 14
Ardan: Latin "passion; eagle"	Feb. 11
Aresius	June 10
Aretas	Oct. 1
Aretius	June 4
Argeus	Jan. 2
Argymirus	June 28
Arian	Mar. 8
Aristaeus	Sept. 3
Aristarchus	Aug. 4
Aristides: Greek "best"	Aug. 31
Aristio	Feb. 22
Aristobulus	Mar. 15
Ariston	July 2
Aristonicus	Apr. 19
Armand: German "strong soldier"	Jan. 23
Armentarius	Jan. 30

Armogastes	Mar. 29
Armon: Hebrew "strong as a fortress; chestnut"	July 31
Arnold: German "ruler; strong; eagle ruler"	Mar. 14
Arnald, Arnaud, Arne: Norse "eagle", **Arno**: Old German "eagle-wolf", **Arnoldo, Arend, Arnoul**	
Arnulf	July 18
Arontius	Aug. 27
Arsacius	Aug. 16
Arsenius: "macho, virile"	July 19
Arsene	
Artemius	Oct. 20
Artemon	Oct. 8
Artemus: Greek "gifted"	Jan. 24
Arthur: English "distinguished"	Dec. 11
Arturo, Artur: Italian "talented"	
Asaph: Hebrew "collector"	May 1
Ascla	Jan. 23
Asclepiades	Oct. 18
Asclepiodotus	Sept. 15
Ashley (Bl. Ralph): English "smooth; ash meadow"	Apr. 7
Aspren	Aug. 3
Asterius	Aug. 23
Astius	July 7
Asyncritus	Apr. 8
Athanasius: Greek "immortal"	May 2
Athenodorus	Oct. 18
Athenogenes	Jan. 18
Atholian	Feb. 6

Attala	Mar. 10
Attalus	June 2
Attho	May 22
Atticus: Greek "ethical", Latin "fron Athens"	Nov. 6
Attilanus	Oct. 5
Attius	Aug. 1
Aubert: German "leader"	Dec. 13
Aubin: French "ruler; elfin"	Mar. 1
Aubrey: English "ruler", Old German "elf; supernatural being, power"	Nov. 14
Auctus	Nov. 7
Audactus	Oct. 24
Audas	May 16
Audax	July 9
Audifax	Jan. 19
Augulus	Feb. 7
Augurius	Jan. 21
Augustalis	Sept. 7
Augustine: Latin "serious and revered"	Aug. 28
Auguste, Augustin, Augustino, Austin: Latin "ingenious", **Austen**	
Augustus: Latin "highly esteemed"	Oct. 7
Aurelian	June 16
Aurelius: Latin "golden son"	July 27
Aureus	June 16
Auspicius	July 8
Austell	June 28
Austregisil	May 20
Austremonius	Nov. 1

Austriclinian	June 30
Authaire	Apr. 24
Authbert	Dec. 13
Autonomus	Sept. 12
Auxanus	Sept. 3
Auxentius	Feb. 14
Auxibius	Feb. 19
Auxilius	Nov. 27
Aventin	Feb. 4
Avitus	Jan. 27
Axel (Alexis): German "peaceful", Hebrew "father of peace"	July 17
Aymar	July 15
Azadan	Apr. 22
Azades	Apr. 22
Azarias	Dec. 16
Azas	Nov. 19

B

Babylas	Jan. 24
Bacchus: Greek "reveler; jaded"	Oct. 7
Bademus	Apr. 10
Badonicus (Gildas)	Jan. 29
Bajulus	Dec. 20
Baldomer	Feb. 27
Baldwin: German "steadfast friend" **Balduin**	July 15
Baltram	Jan. 18
Baptist (St. John): Latin "one who has been baptized; to dip" **Baptiste**	June 24
Barachisius	Mar. 29
Barbabas **Barsabas**	Dec. 11
Barbatian	Dec. 31
Barbatus **Barbas**	Feb. 19
Bardo	June 10
Bardomian	Sept. 25
Barlaam	Nov. 19
Barlow (Bl. Ambrose): English "hardy; the bare hillside"	Sept. 10
Barnabas: Hebrew "seer; son of consolation" **Barnaby**: Hebrew "companionable", **Barney, Barna**	June 11
Barnard	Jan. 23
Barontius	Mar. 25
Barry (Finnbar): Irish "candid; fair-haired" **Barrion, Barr**	Sept. 25

Barsanuphius	Apr. 11
Barsen	Jan. 30
Barsimaeus	Jan. 30
Bartholomew: Hebrew "friendly; earthy; son of the farmer"	Aug. 24

> **Bart**: Hebrew "persistent", **Bartek, Bartel, Barthole, Bathleme, Bartlett, Bartley**: "rural man", **Barton**: Old English "barley settlement", **Bertel, Barto**: Spanish "upward", **Bartolomeo**

Barula	Nov. 18
Basil: Greek "regal"	Jan. 1

> **Basile, Basine**

Basileus	Mar. 2
Basilian	Dec. 18
Basilides	June 10
Basiliscus	Mar. 3
Basolus	Nov. 26
Bassian	Jan. 19
Bassus	Feb. 14
Bastien (Sebastian): Greek "respected"	Jan. 20
Baudelius	May 20
Bavo	Oct. 1
Bean: Scottish "lively"	Dec. 16
Beatus	May 9
Becket (St. Thomas): English "methodical"	Dec. 29
Bede: English "prayerful; prayer bead"	May 27
Bellinus	Nov. 26
Beltram	Mar. 1
Benedict: Latin "blessed man"	Mar. 21

> **Benedic, Bendek, Benedik, Benedicto, Benito**: Italian "blessed", **Bennett**: French "blessed", **Benedetto**

Benignus Feb. 13

Benildes June 15

Benjamin: Hebrew "son of right hand; wonderful boy; son of my old age" Mar. 31

Benno: Italian "wonderful; best" June 16

Benvenuto: Italian "welcomed child" Mar. 22

Berard Jan. 16

Bercharius Oct. 16

Berchmans Aug. 13

Bernard: German "brave and dependable" Aug. 20
> **Barend**: Old German "hard bear", **Barnaro, Berend, Bernal**: Old German "strength of a bear", **Bernardo**: Spanish "brave; bear", **Bernhard, Berns, Burnet**: Old French "brown"

Bernardin May 20
> **Bernardine**

Bernardino July 2

Beronicus Oct. 19

Bertinus Sept. 5

Bertold Oct. 21

Bertran Jan. 24

Bertrand: Old French "bright raven" June 6
> **Bertram**: German "bright, famous raven", **Berton**: Old English "bright settlement", **Bert**: English "shining example; illustrious"

Besas Feb. 27

Bessarion June 17

Beuno Apr. 21
> **Beunor**

Beverly (John B.): English "beaver stream; natural" May 7

Bianor July 10

Biblis June 2

Bicor	Apr. 22
Bill (William): German "strong; resolute"	Jan. 10
Birillus	Mar. 21
Birinus	Dec. 3
Blaise: French "audacious; lisp, stutter"	Feb. 3
Blase, Blaze: Latin "stutter; fire"	
Blandin	May 1
Blane: "svelte"	Aug. 10
Blaine: Irish "svelte"	
Boetius	Oct. 23
Boisil	Feb. 23
Bonajuncta	Aug. 31
Bonaventure: Latin "humble; good fortune"	July 14
Boniface: Latin "fortunate, auspicious; benefactor"	June 5
Bonifaze	
Bonfílius	Jan. 1
Bonitus	Jan. 15
Bononius	Aug. 30
Bonosus	Aug. 21
Bononus	
Bonus	Aug. 1
Boris: Russian "combative; small; battle glory"	July 24
Borromeo (St. Charles)	Nov. 4
Boswell (Boisil): English "well near the woods"	July 7
Brandan: "hill; high-spirited"	Oct. 20
Brannock	Jan. 7
Braulio: Spanish "shining"	Mar. 26
Brendan: Irish "armed; prince"	May 16

Brennan: English "pensive", Irish "teardrop"   May 6

Bretannio   Jan. 25

Brian: Irish "strong man of honor; noble"   Mar. 22
    Brien, Bryan

Briant (Bl. Alex)   Dec. 1

Brice: Welsh "go-getter"   Nov. 13

Brictius   July 9

Brinstan   Nov. 4
    Bristan

Brittan   May 19

Brogan: Irish "sturdy shoe; dependable"   Sept. 17

Bruce (Ambrose): French "complicated; from a thicket of brushwood"   Dec. 7

Bruno: German "brown"   Oct. 6

Burton (Bertinus): English "protective; fortified settlement"   Sept. 5

Byron (Birinus): English "reclusive; small cottage; at the byres or barn"   Dec. 3

C

Cadoc	Jan. 24
Cadocus	
Cadwallader	Nov. 12
Caecilius	June 3
Caelian	Dec. 15
Caerealis	Feb. 28
Caesar: Latin "focused leader; head of hair"	Aug. 27
Cesar	
Caesareus	Apr. 20
Caesarius	Dec. 28
Caesidius	Aug. 31
Cahil (Charles)	Nov. 4
Caius: Latin "rejoice"	Jan. 4
Cajetan: Italian "from Gaeta"	Aug. 7
Calanicus	Dec. 17
Caleb: Hebrew "faithful; brave; dog"	Oct. 27
Caleposius	May 10
Calimerius	July 31
Calixtus	Oct. 14
Callen	Nov. 28
Callinicus	Jan. 28
Calliopius	Apr. 7
Callistratus	Sept. 26
Callistus	Apr. 16
Calocerus	Apr. 18

Calogerus	June 18
Camerinus	Aug. 21
Camillus	July 14
Camille, Comillo	
Campion (Bl. Edmund): English "champion"	Dec. 1
Candidus	Feb. 2
Canion	Sept. 1
Cantian	May 31
Cantidian	Aug. 5
Cantidius	Aug. 5
Cantius	May 31
Canute: Scandinavian: "great; knot"	Jan. 7
Canut, Cnud	
Canutus	Jan. 19
Capito	Mar. 4
Caprasius	June 1
Caralippus	Apr. 28
Caraunus	May 28
Carponius	Oct. 14
Carpophorus	Aug. 7
Carpus	Apr. 13
Carterius	Nov. 2
Carter: English "insightful; one who transports goods"	
Cary: English "pretty brook; charming", Celtic "hill fort"	Jan. 3
Casimir: Polish "peace-loving"	Mar. 4
Casmir	
Casper: German "secretive"	Jan. 28
Caspar	

Cass: Irish "funny" — Aug. 13

Cassian — Mar. 26

Cassius: Latin "protective" — June 29

Castor: Greek "eager protector" — Mar. 28

Castorius — July 7

Castrensis — Feb. 11

Castritian — Dec. 1

Castulus — Jan. 12

Castus — May 22

Cataldus — May 10

Cato: Latin "zany and bright; all-knowing" — Dec. 28

Catulinus — July 15

Caturninus — Feb. 6

Catus — Jan. 19

Cecil: Latin "unseeing; hard-headed; blind" — Feb. 1

Cecilian — Apr. 16

Cecilius — June 3

Cedd — Jan. 7

Celerinus — Feb. 3

Celestine — July 27

Celsus — Jan. 9

Censurius — June 10

Ceolfrid — Sept. 25

Cerbonius — Oct. 10

Chad: English "firebrand" — Mar. 2
    Ceada

Chaeremon — Oct. 4

Charisius	Aug. 22
Charistius	Apr. 16
Chariton	Sept. 3
Charles: German "manly; well-loved; free man"	Nov. 4

    Cahil, Carel, Carol: Irish "champion", **Carl**: English "masculine", **Carlo**: Italian "sensual; manly", **Carlos**: Spanish "manly; sensual", **Charlet, Charlot, Carlton**: Old English "free peasant settlement"

Cheledonius	Mar. 3
Chester (Ceslaus): English "camp of soldiers; comfy-cozy"	July 17
Christian: Latin "follower of Christ"	Nov. 12
Christopher: Greek "the bearer of Christ"	July 25

    Christophe: French "beloved of Christ", **Christot, Chris**: Greek "close to Christ"

Chrodegang	Mar. 6
Chromatius	Dec. 2
Chronides	Mar. 27
Chrysanthus	Oct. 25
Chrysogonus	Nov. 24
Chrysophorus	Apr. 20
Chrysostom	Jan. 27
Chrysotelus	Apr. 22
Cindeus	July 11
Ciro (Cyriac): Italian "lordly", Spanish "sun; throne"	Aug. 8
Cisellus	Aug. 21
Clarence: Latin "intelligent"	Apr. 26
Claret (Bl. Anthony)	Oct. 24
Clarus	Nov. 4

    Clair: English "renowned", Latin "bright"

Classicus	Feb. 18

Clateus	June 4
Claud	June 6
Claude: Latin "slow-moving; lame", **Claudio**	
Claudian	Feb. 25
Claudius	Feb. 18
Claus (Nicholas): Greek "victorious"	Dec. 6
Clement: Scottish "gentle", Latin "merciful"	Jan. 23
Clem: Latin "casual", **Clemence, Clemento, Clemente**: Spanish "pleasant"	
Clementinus	Nov. 14
Cleonicus	Mar. 3
Cleophas: Greek "seeing glory; known"	Sept. 25
Clerus	Jan. 7
Cletus: Greek "creative; invoked"	Apr. 26
Clicerius	Sept. 20
Clinius	Mar. 30
Clodulph	June 8
Cloud	Sept. 7
Clovis (Louis): German "famed warrior"	Aug. 25
Codratus	Mar. 10
Colan	May 21
Colin (Nicholas): Irish "young and quiet; peaceful; the people's victor"	Dec. 6
Colman	Oct. 13
Coleman (Bl. Edward)	Dec. 1
Colum: Latin "peaceful; dove"	Sept. 22
Columba	June 9
Columkille	

Columbanus	Nov. 21
Columban	
Conald	Sept. 24
Conan: Irish "worthy of praise; hound, wolf"	Mar. 8
Concessus	Apr. 9
Concordius: "agreeable"	Jan. 1
Conon	Feb. 26
Conrad: German "optimist; brave, bold leader"	Apr. 21
Court: German "eloquent"	
Constantine: Latin "consistent"	July 27
Curt: French "kind"	
Constantius	Jan. 29
Consul	July 7
Copres	July 9
Corbinian: Latin "crow, raven"	Sept. 8
Corebus	Apr. 18
Cormac: Irish "the raven's offspring; watchful; impure son"	Sept. 14
Cornelius: Greek "a temptation", Latin "horn"	Feb. 2
Corney, Corneille	
Cosmas: Greek "universal"	Sept. 27
Cosmo: Greek "in harmony with life"	
Cottidus	Sept. 6
Craton	Feb. 15
Credan	Aug. 19
Crementius	Apr. 16
Crescens	Mar. 10
Crescentian	May 31
Crescentio	Sept. 17
Crescention	

Crescentius Apr. 19
    Crescent

Cresconius Nov. 28

Crispin: Latin "man with curls" Jan. 7

Crispinian Oct. 25

Crispulus May 30

Crispus Aug. 18

Cronan Apr. 28

Ctesiphon May 15

Cucuphas July 25

Cullan: "attractive" May 21

Culmatius June 19

Cunibert Nov. 12

Curcodomus May 4

Curonotus Sept. 12

Cuthbert: English "intelligent, famous" Mar. 20

Cuthman Feb. 8

Cutias Feb. 18

Cyprian Sept. 16
    Cyprien: French "religious"

Cyr June 16
    Cyrano: Greek "shy heart", **Cyran, Cyrin**

Cyriac Dec. 19

Cyriacus Jan. 31

Cyricus June 16

Cyril: Greek "regal; master, lord" Jan. 28
    Cyrill, Cyrille, Cirilo

Cyrinus Jan. 3

Cyrion	Feb. 14
Cyrus: Persian "sunny"	Jan. 31
Cythinus	July 17

D

Dacian	June 4
Dacius	Nov. 1
Dadas: African "curly-haired"	Apr. 13
Dalmatius	Dec. 5
Damarius: "tamer of wild things"	Sept. 30
Damasus	Dec. 11
Damian: Greek "fate"; Latin "demon" **Damien, Damio**	Sept. 27
Daniel: Hebrew "God is my judge; spiritual" **Danil, Dannel, Danny**	Jan. 3
Darius: Greek "affluent, rich, kingly"	Dec. 19
Dasius	Oct. 21
Dathus	July 3
Datius	Jan. 14
Dativus	Jan. 27
David: Hebrew "beloved" **Dawid, Dave, Davie**	Dec. 29
Davinus	June 3
Davitus	Feb. 11
Declan: Irish "strong; prayerful"	July 24
Decorosus	Feb. 15
Dedric (Theodoric): German "leader"	July 1
Deicola	Jan. 18
Deiphinus	Dec. 24
Demetrius	Apr. 9
Democritus	July 31

Denis: Greek "reveler"	Feb. 8
Dennis, Denez, Dennet, Denys, Dinis	
Deodatus	Apr. 24
Deogratius	Mar. 22
Dermit	Mar. 2
Dermot: Irish "unabashed; giving; free man"	Jan. 18
Desiderius: "desirable"	Feb. 11
Desire (Desiderius): "desirable"	Sept. 16
Deusdedit	Aug. 10
Devereaux: French "divine"	Nov. 14
Devereau	
Dewey (David): Welsh "valued"	Mar. 1
Dexter: Latin "skillful; right-handed"	May 7
Diago (James)	July 25
Diego: Spanish "untamed; wild"	
Didacus	Nov. 12
Didius	Nov. 26
Didymus	Apr. 28
Dietrich (Theobald): German "ruler"	June 30
Diocles	May 24
Diocletius	May 11
Diodorus	Jan. 17
Diogenes: Greek "honest man"	Apr. 6
Diomede	Aug. 16
Diomedes	Sept. 2
Dion: Greek "reveler"	July 6
Dionysius: Greek "joyous celebrant"	Oct. 9
Dioscorides	May 10

Dioscorus	Feb. 25
Dolph (Adolph): German "noble wolf"	Sept. 27
Dometius	Aug. 7
Dominator	Nov. 5
Dominic: Latin "child of the Lord"	Jan. 22
Domitian	July 1
Domitius	Mar. 23
Domninus	Mar. 21
Domnio	Apr. 11
Domnolus	May 16
Domnus	Oct. 10
Donatian	May 24
Donatus	Jan. 25
Dorotheus: "gift from God"	Sept. 9
Dorymedon	Sept. 19
Dreux	Apr. 16
Droctoveus	Mar. 10
Drogo	Apr. 16
Drusus	Dec. 14
Duane: Irish "dark man, swarthy"	Feb. 11
Dulas	June 15
Dunstan: English "brown stone; well-girded"	May 19
Durban (Urban) **Durbin**: Latin "city dweller"	May 25
Durdan	Sept. 5
Dustan: "bold and brave"	July 11

E

Eadbert	May 6
Eagan: Irish "intense; fiery"	May 31
Eamon (Edmund): Irish "thriving; protective"	Nov. 16
Earl (Herluin): English "promising; noble"	Aug. 26
Ebruif	Dec. 29
Edbert: German "courageous", English "wealthy and bright"	May 6
Edfrid	Oct. 26
Edgar: English "success; wealthy spear"	July 8
Edistius	Oct. 12
Edmund: English "protective", German "wealthy guard" **Edmond**	Nov. 16
Ednyfed	May 21
Edwald	Mar. 23
Edward: English "prospering; defender" **Edsel**: Old English "noble; bright; wealthy man's house", **Edson, Eduard, Edvard**	Jan. 5
Edwin: English "prosperous friend"	Oct. 12
Egbert: English "brilliant sword"	Apr. 24
Egdunus	Mar. 12
Elbert (Albert): English "highborn; shining"	Nov. 15
Eldred: English "wise advisor"	Mar. 13
Eleazar: Hebrew "helped by God"	Aug. 23
Elesbaan	Oct. 27
Eleuchadius	Feb. 14
Eleusippus	Jan. 17
Eleutherius	Feb. 20

Elgar: "of noble birth"	June 14
Elias: Greek "spiritual"	July 20
Ellis, Eliot, Elliott: English "God-loving"	
Eligius	Dec. 1
Eliphius	Oct. 16
Eliseus	June 14
Elmer: English "famed; noble"	Aug. 28
Elmo: Greek "gregarious", Latin "God's helmet; amiable"	June 2
Elphege	Apr. 19
Elpiderphorus	Nov. 2
Elpidius	Mar. 4
Elvis: Scandinavian "wise; musical"	Feb. 22
Elwin: English "friend of elves"	Feb. 22
Elzear	Sept. 27
Emeric	Nov. 4
Emery: German "hardworking leader; home strength"	
Emil: Latin "ingratiating; eager"	Feb. 1
Emile	
Emilas	Sept. 15
Emilian	Nov. 12
Emmanuel: Hebrew "with God"	Mar. 26
Emanuel, Emminuel	
Emmeramus	Sept. 22
Emmeram	
Emmeric	Nov. 4
Emory	
Emygdius	Aug. 5
Eneco	June 1
Engelbert: German "angel-bright"	Nov. 7

Ennodius	July 17
Enoch: Hebrew "dedicated instructor; trained and vowed; profound"	Mar. 26
Enos: Hebrew "mortal"	May 1
Enrico (Henry): Italian "ruler" **Enzio**	July 15
Eobanus	June 5
Epagathus	June 2
Epaphras	July 19
Epaphroditus	Mar. 22
Eparchius	Mar. 23
Ephebus	Feb. 14
Ephisius	Jan. 15
Ephraem	Mar. 4
Ephrem: Hebrew "fertile"	June 18
Epictetus	Jan. 9
Epigmenius	Mar. 24
Epimachus	Dec. 12
Epiphanius	Jan. 21
Epipodius	Apr. 22
Epitacius	May 23
Epolonius	Jan. 24
Equitius	Aug. 11
Erasmus: Greek "beloved"	June 2
Erastus: Greek "loved baby; loving"	July 26
Erhard: German "strong resolve"	Jan. 8
Eric: Scandinavian "powerful leader" **Erich, Erick, Erik**	May 18

Erkonwald   Apr. 30
     Erkenwald, Erconwald

Ermin: German "soldier"   Apr. 25

Ernest: English "sincere"   Nov. 7
     Ernesto: Spanish "sincere", **Ernst, Erneste**

Erotis   Oct. 6

Ervan (Ervin)   May 29

Esdras   July 13

Esme (Osmund): French "beloved"   Dec. 4

Esteban (Stephan): Spanish "royal; friendly"   Feb. 8
     Etienne: French "crown"

Ethbin   Oct. 19

Ethelbert: German "principled; highborn; shining"   Feb. 24

Ethelwold   Aug. 1

Etherius (Aetherius)   June 14

Ethian (Ethern)   May 27

Eubulus   Mar. 7

Eucarpius   Mar. 18

Eucarpus   Sept. 25

Eucharius   Dec. 8

Eucherius   Feb. 20

Eudoxius   Sept. 5

Eudus (Otto)   Jan. 16

Eugendus   Jan. 1

Eugene: Greek "blue-blood"   Jan. 4
     Eugen, Eugenio

Eugenian   Jan. 8

Eugenius   Jan. 4

Eugraphus	Dec. 10
Eulampius	Oct. 10
Eulogius	Jan. 21
Eumenius	Sept. 18
Eumenes	
Eunicianus	Dec. 23
Eunician	
Eunus	Oct. 30
Euphebius	May 23
Euphrasius	Jan. 14
Euphronius	Aug. 3
Euplius	Aug. 12
Euporus	Dec. 23
Euprepis	Nov. 30
Euprepius	Aug. 21
Eupsychius	Sept. 7
Eusebius: "devoted to God"	June 21
Eusignius	Aug. 5
Eustace: Latin "calming", Greek "bountiful grapes"	Sept. 20
Eustachius, Eustis	
Eustasius	Mar. 29
Eustathius	July 28
Eusterius	Oct. 19
Eustochius	Sept. 19
Eustorgius	Apr. 11
Eustosius	Nov. 10
Eustratius	Dec. 13
Euthymius	Jan. 20

Eutropius	Jan. 12
Eutyches	Apr. 15
Eutychian	July 2
Eutychius	Feb. 4
Evagrius	Mar. 6
Evan: Irish "warrior", Welsh "the Lord is gracious"	Aug. 18
Evaristus	Oct. 14
Evasius	Dec. 1
Evelius	May 11
Evelyn: American "writer"	Dec. 19
Eventius	Apr. 16
Evergislus	Oct. 24
Everistus	Dec. 23
Evilasius	Sept. 20
Evodius	Apr. 25
Evortius	Sept. 7
Ewald: Polish "fair ruler", English "law-powerful"	Oct. 3
Exanthus	Aug. 7
Expeditus	Apr. 19
Exuperantius	Jan. 24
Exuperius	May 2
Ezechiel: Hebrew "God's strength"	Apr. 10
Ezekiel: Hebrew "strength of God"	
Ezra: Hebrew "helpful; strong"	July 13

F

Fabian: Latin "grower; singer"	Jan. 20
Fabien: French	
Fabius	May 11
Fabrician	Aug. 22
Facundus	Nov. 27
Falco: Latin	Feb. 20
Fandila	June 13
Fantinus	Aug. 30
Farrel (Fergus): "brave"	Nov. 18
Faro: Italian "grain"	Oct. 28
Faustinian	Feb. 26
Faustinus	Feb. 15
Faustus	June 24
Fedor (Theodore): German "romantic", Greek "gift from God"	Jan. 7
Felician	Jan. 24
Felicianus	June 9
Felicíssimus	May 26
Felinus	June 1
Felix: Latin "joyful, fortunate"	Jan. 7
Felice	
Felipe (Phillip): Spanish "horse-lover"	May 1
Felton (Bl. John): English "farming the field"	Aug. 8
Ferdinand: German: "adventurer"	May 30
Fernando: Spanish "bold leader", **Ferrante, Ferd, Ferde**	
Fergus: Irish, Scottish "supreme man; highest choice"	Mar. 29

Ferreol	June 16
Ferreolus	
Ferruntion	June 16
Ferrutio	
Ferrutius	Oct. 28
Festus: Latin "joyous, festive"	Sept. 19
Fiacre	Aug. 30
Fibitius	Nov. 5
Fidelis: Latin "faithful"	Apr. 24
Fidentian	Nov. 15
Fidentius	Sept. 27
Fidolus	May 16
Filbert (Philbert): English "genius"	Aug. 20
Filipe (Philip): "horse-lover"	May 1
Fillipo	
Finbarr: Irish "blond"	Sept. 25
Fingar	Dec. 14
Finian: Irish "fair"	Oct. 21
Fintan: Irish "little fair one"	Feb. 17
Firmatus	Oct. 5
Firmin: French "loyal"	Mar. 11
Firminus	June 24
Firmus	Feb. 2
Flavian: Greek "blond"	Jan. 28
Flavius	May 7
Flobert	Dec. 31
Flocellus	Sept. 17

Florentius **Florentine**	Jan. 3
Florens	Dec. 29
Florian: Latin "flourishing; flower"	May 4
Florius	Oct. 26
Florus	Aug. 18
Flos	Dec. 31
Flosculus	Feb. 2
Floyd (Florentius): English "practical; hair of gray"	June 9
Forde: English "strong"	May 28
Fortis	May 9
Fortunatus	Jan. 9
Foster (Vedast): Latin "worthy", Old English "woodsman"	Feb. 6
Francis: Latin "free-spirit"	Oct. 4

   Franchon, Franc, Francisco: Spanish, **Franco**: Spanish "defender; spear", **Francois**: French "smooth; patriot; Frenchman", **Franek, Frank**: "outspoken; landowner", **Franz**: German "man from France; free", **Franklin**: English "outspoken; landowner"

Fraternus	Sept. 29
Frederick: German "plainspoken leader; peaceful"	July 18

   Fred, Frederic: French "peaceful king", **Frederico, Fritz**

Freeman (Bl. William): English "free man"	Aug. 18
Frementius	Mar. 23
Fridian	Mar. 18
Frigidian **Frigdian**	Nov. 18
Fronto	Apr. 14
Froylan	Oct. 3
Fructulus	Feb. 18

Fructuosus	Jan. 21
Frumentius	Oct. 27
Fulgentius: Latin "full of kindness; shines"	Jan. 1
Fulk: English "folksy"	Oct. 26
Fursey: Irish "spiritual"	Jan. 16
Fuscian	Dec. 11
Fusculus	Sept. 6

G

Gabdelas	Sept. 29
Gabinus	May 30
Gabriel: Hebrew "God's hero; devout; able-bodied one"	Mar. 24
Gabrielo, Gavril: Hebrew "strong"	
Galatas	Apr. 19
Galation	Nov. 5
Galdini	Apr. 18
Galdinus	
Galen: Greek "healer; physician; tranquil"	June 22
Galganus	Dec. 3
Gall	Oct. 16
Gallus	
Gallan	Dec. 7
Gallicanus	June 25
Gallican	
Gamaliel: Hebrew "rewarded by God"	Aug. 3
Gangulphus	May 11
Gangulph	
Garcia: Spanish "strong"	Feb. 5
Gardiner (Bl. George): English "keeper of the garden"	Mar. 7
Garibaldi	Jan. 8
Garnier	July 19
Gaspar: "he who guards the treasure"	Dec. 28
Gaston: French "native of Gascony; stranger"	Feb. 6
Gatian	Dec. 18
Gaudentius	Jan. 22
Gaudens	

Gaudiosus	Mar. 7
Gaugericus	Aug. 11
Gaugeric	
Gautier	Apr. 9
Gavinus	Feb. 19
Gedeon: Hebrew "power-wielding"	Sept. 1
Gideon: Hebrew "feller of trees"	
Gelasius	Feb. 4
Gemellus	Dec. 10
Geminian	Jan. 31
Geminus	Jan. 4
Gene (Eugene): Greek "noble"	Mar. 3
Generalis	Sept. 14
Generosus	July 17
Genesius	Aug. 25
Gennadius	May 16
Gentian	Dec. 11
Genuinus	Feb. 5
Geoffrey (Godfrey): English "peaceful"	Nov. 8
George: Greek "land-loving; farmer"	Apr. 23
Georg: German "works with the earth", **Georgt, Giorgio**: Italian "earthy; creative", **Gorg**	
Gerald: German "strong; ruling with a spear"	Oct. 13
Gerry, Girald, Garret, Garrett: Irish "brave; watchful"	
Gerard: English "spear brave"	Oct. 16
Geraud, Gerhard: German "forceful", **Giraud**	
Gerasimus	Mar. 5
Geremarus	Sept. 24
Geremar	

Gereon	Oct. 10
Gerinus	Oct. 2
German: German: "from the country of Germany"	Feb. 21
Germanicus	Jan. 19
Germanus	May 2
Gerold: Danish "rules with spears"	Apr. 19
Geronimo (Jerome): Italian "wild heart"	Sept. 30
Gerontius: Latin "old man"	Jan. 19
Geruntius	May 5
Gervase: French "man of honor" **Gervasius**	June 19
Gery (Gaudric)	Aug. 11
Getulius	June 10
Gilbert: French "bright promise" **Gilberto**: Spanish "bright"**, Gisbert**	Feb. 4
Gildard	June 8
Gildas	Jan. 29
Giles: French "protective", Greek "small goat" **Gilles, Gillet, Gil**: "happy man"	Sept. 1
Giovanni (John): Italian "the Lord is gracious"	Dec. 27
Girard	Dec. 29
Gislenus	Oct. 9
Giuseppe (Joseph): Italian "capable; the Lord increases"	Mar. 19
Glycerius	Dec. 21
Goar	July 6
Goddard: German "staunch in spirituality" **Godard**	May 4

Godfrey: Irish "peaceful", German "God-peace" Nov. 8
  Giotto, Gottfried

Godrick: English "man of God" May 21

Godwin: English "close to God" Oct. 28
  Goodwin: Old English "good friend"

Gonzaga June 21

Gordian Sept. 17
  Gordien

Gordius Jan. 3
  Gordon: English "nature-lover; hill"

Gorgonius Sept. 9

Gorman: Irish "small blue-eyed one" Aug. 28

Gothard May 4
  Godard

Gottschalk June 7

Gratian Dec. 18

Gratinian June 1

Gratus Dec. 5

Gregory: Greek "watchful, vigilant" Mar. 12
  Gregor, Gregus, Gregorio: Italian "careful", **Gregoire**: French
  "watchful", **Gregg**: Latin "vigilant"

Griffith: Welsh "able leader" July 1

Grimoaldus Sept. 29
  Grimoald

Guarian July 27

Guarinus Feb. 6

Guido: Italian "guiding" Sept. 12

Guillaume (William): French "will helmet, protection" Jan. 10

Gumesind Jan. 13

Gummarus **Gummar**	Oct. 11
Gundulphus **Gundulph**	June 17
Gunifort	Aug. 22
Gunther: Scandinavian "able fighter"	Sept. 9
Guntram	Mar. 28
Gurias	Nov. 15
Gus (Augustine): Latin "worthy of respect"	Aug. 28
Gustave (Augustus): Scandinavian "royal staff"	Oct. 7
Guy: French "assertive", German "leader; wood" **Guidon, Guyon**	Sept. 12

H

Habacuc	Jan. 15
Habert	Dec. 19
Habentius	June 7
Hadrian (Adrian): Roman "from Hadria"	Mar. 4
Hansel (John): Scandinavian "gullible; open"	Dec. 27
Happy (Felix)	May 30
Harding (Bl. Stephen): English "fiery; son of the courageous one"	Apr. 17
Harold: Scandinavian "leader of an army"	Mar. 25
Hart (Bl. William): English "giving; strong, brave; stag"	Mar. 13
Harvey: German "fighter", English "eager for battle; strong and worthy"	Feb. 17
Harward **Harwarld**	Sept. 16
Hegesippus	Apr. 7
Helanus	Oct. 7
Helimenas	Apr. 22
Heliodorus	May 6
Helladius	Jan. 8
Henry: German "leader; estate ruler" **Hawkins**: Old English "little hawk", **Henning**: Scandinavian "ruler", **Hendrik**: German "home ruler", **Henriot, Henryk, Heinrich**: German "leader", **Hal**: English "home ruler", **Harry**: English "home ruler"	July 15
Heracleas	Sept. 29
Heracles	July 14
Heraclides	June 28
Heraclius	Mar. 2
Heradius	May 17

Herbert: Old German "illustrious warrior"	Mar. 20
Herculanus	Mar. 1
Herenas	Feb. 25
Herena	
Heribert: German ·	Mar. 16
Hermagoras	July 12
Herman: Latin "fair fighter; soldier"	Apr. 7
Hermangild	Apr. 13
Hermenegild	
Hermas	May 9
Hermeland	Mar. 25
Hermellus	Aug. 3
Hermengaud	Nov. 3
Hermengaudius	
Hermes: Greek "courier of messages"	Jan. 4
Hermias	May 31
Hermippus	July 27
Hermiterius	Mar. 3
Hermocrates	July 27
Hermogenes	Apr. 25
Hermolaus	July 27
Hermylus	Jan. 13
Hero	June 24
Heros	
Herodian	Apr. 8
Heron	June 28
Herundo	July 23
Hesychius	May 15

Hiero   Nov. 7
   Hieron

Hieronides   Sept. 12

Hierotheus   Oct. 4

Hilarinus   July 16

Hilarion: Greek "cheery; hilarious"   Oct. 21

Hilary: Latin "joyful; cheerful; happy"   Jan. 14
   Hilaire, Hilario, Hilarus

Hildebrand: German "combative; battle sword"   May 25

Himerius   June 17

Hippolytus: "free horses"   Jan. 30

Hirenarchus   Nov. 27

Hobart (Hubert): German "bright or shining intellect"   Nov. 3

Hodge (Robert): English form of Roger, "vibrant"   May 13

Homobonus   Nov. 13

Honoratus   Jan. 16

Honorius   Sept. 30

Hormisdas   Aug 6

Horres   Mar. 13

Hortulanus   Nov. 28
   Hortulan

Hospitius   May 21

Howard (Bl. William): English "well-liked; noble watchman"   Dec. 29

Howell (Hywell): Welsh "outstanding; eminent"   Jan. 6

Hubert: German "intellectual"   Nov. 3
   Hubbard: German "fine"

Hudson (Bl. James): English "Hugh's son; charismatic adventurer"   Nov. 28

Hugh: English "intelligent"; German "soul, mind, intellect"   Apr. 1
     Hugo: Latin "spirited heart", **Hughes, Hutchin**

Humbert: Old German "famous giant; renowned warrior"   Mar. 4

Humphrey: German "strong peacemaker; peaceful warrior"   Mar. 8
     Humphry

Hyacinth: French "flowering"   Aug. 16
     Hyacinthe: French "hyacinth"

Hyacinthus   Sept. 11

Hyginus   Jan. 11

Hypatius   June 3

I

Iago (James): Spanish "feisty villain; he who supplants"   July 25

Ian (John): Scottish "believer; handsome; God is gracious"   Dec. 27

Ignatius: Latin "firebrand; ardent; burning"   Feb. 1
     Ignace, Ignacy, Ignazio

Igor: Russian "warrior"   June 5

Ildefonse   Jan. 23

Illidius   July 7

Illuminatus   May 11

Imbert   Sept. 6

Immanuel: Hebrew "honored; with us is God"   July 10

Indaletius   May 15

Indes   Dec. 28

Ingen   Dec. 20

Innocent   July 28

Irenaeus   Feb. 10

Irenion   Dec. 16

Irvin (Urban): English "attractive"   May 25
     Irving: English "attractive; sea friend"

Isaac: Hebrew "laughter"   Apr. 11

Isacius   Apr. 21

Isaias: Hebrew "saved by God"   July 6

Isaurus   June 17

Ischyrion   Dec. 22

Isidore: Greek, French "gift"   Jan. 2
     Isidro

Ismael   June 17

Israel: Hebrew "God's prince; God perseveres, contends"   Dec. 22

Ivan: Russian "reliable one; God is gracious"   June 24

Ives   Apr. 24

Ivo: Polish "yew tree; sturdy; archer's bow"   May 19
    Ivar: "outgoing; ready"

J

Jacinte (Hyacinth)	Aug. 16
Jacob: Hebrew "he who supplants; best boy"	Dec. 19
Jader	Sept. 10
James: English "dependable; steadfast"	July 25

    Jacques: French "romantic; ingenious", **Jago:** English "self-assured", **Jaime:** Spanish "follower", **Jamek, Jamnik, Jayme**

Januarius	Jan. 7
Jared: Hebrew "descendant; giving"	Mar. 1
Jareth: American "open to adventure"	Oct. 27
Jarett (Gerald): English "confident"	Oct. 13
Jarlath	Feb. 11
Jarmin	Feb. 23
Jason: Greek "healer; man on a quest; the Lord is salvation"	July 12
Jasper (Caspar): English "guard; country boy; treasure holder"	Dec. 28
Jeffrey (Godfrey): English "peaceful"	Nov. 8

    Jeffry, Joffre: German "bright star"

Jeremias: Hebrew "prophet uplifted by God; far-sighted"	May 1

    Jeremy: English "talkative"

Jerome: Latin "holy name; blessed; sacred name"	July 20

    Jeronimo: Italian "excited", **Jerom**

Jesse: Hebrew "the Lord exists; wealthy"	Dec. 29

Jesus: Hebrew "the Lord is salvation"

    *Most cultures do not give Our Lord's name in baptism to their children out of reverence for Our Lord.

Joachim: Hebrew "a king of Judah; powerful; believer; established by God"

Joaquin: Spanish "bold; hip"	Aug. 16
Joannicius	Nov. 4

    Joannicus

Jocelyn	Mar. 17
Josselin	
Job: Hebrew "patient; persecuted"	May 10
Joel: Hebrew "Jehovah is the Lord"	July 13
John: Hebrew "honorable; the Lord is gracious"	Dec. 27
Jan: Dutch "believer", **Johan, Johann**: German "spiritual musician", **Juan**: Spanish "devout; lively", **Janek**	
Jonas: Hebrew "capable; active"	Feb. 11
Jordan: Hebrew "descending"	Feb. 15
Joris (George)	Apr. 23
Jurgen: Scandinavian "farmer"	
Josaphat	Nov. 12
Joseph: Hebrew "asset; Jehovah increases"	Mar. 19
Jose: Spanish "asset; favored", **Josef, Jozef**: Polish "supported by Jehovah; asset"	
Josue: Spanish "devout"	Sept. 1
Jovian	June 1
Jovinian	May 5
Jovinus	Mar. 26
Jovita	Feb. 15
Joyce	Dec. 13
Jucundian	July 4
Jucundinus	July 21
Jucundus	Jan. 9
Jude: Latin "praised"	Oct. 28
Judoc	Dec. 13
Julian: Greek "gorgeous"	Jan. 7
Julien	

Julius: Greek "attractive"   Jan. 19
    Jules

Junius: Latin "young"   May 17

Justin: Latin "fair; just, upright, righteous"   Jan. 1

Justus: German "fair; just"   Nov. 10

Juvenal: Latin "young"   May 3

Juventius   Jan. 25

K

Kanut (Canute)	Jan. 7
Karl (Charles): Scandinavian "hair curls", German "free man" **Karol, Karel**	Nov. 4
Kasimir (Casimir): Slavic, Arabic "serene"	Mar. 4
Kaspar (Caspar): German "reliable; keeper of the treasure" **Kasper, Kass**: German "standout among men"	Dec. 28
Kelan (Callen)	Nov. 28
Kellen: Irish "strong-willed", Gaelic "slender"	Mar. 26
Kellog	Apr. 1
Kemble (Bl. John)	Aug. 22
Kenelm: English "handsome boy; brave helmet"	July 17
Kennan **Kenan**: Hebrew "acquire"	Feb. 25
Kenneth: Scottish "handsome," Irish "good-looking; fire born" **Kenny, Kenzie**: Scottish "leads"	Oct. 11
Kent (Kentigern): English "fair-skinned; edge"	Jan. 14
Kernan	Nov. 5
Kerstan (Christian)	Apr. 18
Kevin (Keevin): Irish "handsome beloved; gentle"	June 3
Kieran: Irish "handsome brunette; black" **Kiaran**	Sept. 9
Kilian	July 8
Killian: Irish "small, fierce; effervescent" **Kim** (Korean martyrs): Vietnamese "precious metal; gold," English "enthusiastic"	Nov. 13
Klas (Nicholas): German "wealthy" **Klaas, Klaus**: "victorious people"	Dec. 6
Knute (Canute): Scandinavian "aggressive; knot"	Jan. 7

Konrad: German, Polish "bold advisor"   Feb. 19

Kristopher: Greek "bearer of Christ"   July 25

Kurt (Constantine): German "wise advisor"   July 27

L

Lacy (Bl. William): Scottish "warlike"	Aug. 22
Ladislaus	June 27
Ladislas: Slavic "glorious rule"	
Laetantius	July 17
Laetus	Sept. 1
Lambert: German "bright", Scandinavian "land brilliant"	Apr. 14
Lamberto, Lambrecht	
Lancelot: French "servant"	June 27
Lance: French "land"	
Landelin	June 15
Landert	Sept. 17
Landoald	Mar. 19
Landry: French "entrepreneur"	Apr. 17
Lanfranc	June 23
Lanto	Sept. 22
Largus	Aug. 8
Latinus	Mar. 24
Laurentinus	Feb. 3
Laurian	July 4
Laurus	Aug. 18
Lawrence: Latin "honored; from Laurentum"	Jan. 8
Laurence: Latin "glorified", **Lars**: Scandinavian, **Larkin**: Irish "brash", **Larse, Lauren, Lauritz, Loren**: Latin "hopeful; winning", **Lorenz, Lorenzo**: Italian, Spanish "bold and spirited", **Lorin, Lorus, Lawrie**: Latin "anointed"	
Lazarus: Greek "renewed", Hebrew "God is my help"	Feb. 11
Lazar: Hebrew "helped by God", **Lazare, Lazaro**	
Leander: Greek "ferocious; lion-like"	Feb. 27

Leo: Latin "lion-like; fierce"   Feb. 20
    Leon: Greek "tenacious", **Lionel:** French "fierce", **Lee:** English
    "loving; pasture or meadow"

Leobard   Jan. 18

Leobinus   Sept. 15
    Leobin

Leodegarius   Oct. 2
    Leodegar

Leomines   Dec. 23

Leonard: German "courageous, lion strength"   Nov. 26
    Leonardo: Italian "lion-hearted", **Lenny:** German

Leonides   Jan. 28

Leontius   Jan. 13

Leopardus   Sept. 30

Leopold: German "brave"   Nov. 15

Leovigild   Aug. 20

Lester (Slyvester): Old English "from Leicester"   Dec. 31

Leucian   Dec. 24

Leucius   Jan. 11

Leutfrid   June 21

Levi: Hebrew "joined; harmonious"   Dec. 22

Liberatus   Aug. 17

Liberius   Dec. 30

Libertus   Dec. 20

Liborius   July 23

Licarion   June 7

Licerius   Aug. 27

Licinius   Aug. 7

Lifard	June 3
Ligorius	Sept. 13
Liguori (St. Alphonsus)	Aug. 2
Linus: Greek "blond, flax"	Sept. 23
Lipo (Philip)	May 1
Litteus	Sept. 10
Livinus	Nov. 12
Llewelyn: English "fiery; fast" **Llywelen**	Apr. 7
Lochen	June 12
Lockwood (Bl. John): Old English "forest near the fortified place"	Apr. 13
Longinus	Mar. 15
Loran	Aug. 30
Lorgius	Mar. 2
Lothaire: German "lover" **Lothar**: Old German "famous warrior"	June 14
Loughlan (Malachy)	Jan. 14
Louis: German, French "powerful ruler" **Lewis**: English "renowned fighter", **Loiz, Luigi**: Italian "famed warrior", **Luis**: Spanish "outspoken"	Aug. 25
Loyola (St. Ignatius) **Lyle**: French "unique; the island"	July 31
Lucanus **Lucan**: Irish "light; from Lucania"	Oct. 30
Lucas: Greek "creative"	June 27
Lucian: Latin "soothing; light" **Lucien**	Jan. 7
Lucillian	June 3
Luciolus	Mar. 3

Lucius: Latin "sunny"   Feb. 8

Ludger: Scandinavian "wielding"   Mar. 26

Ludwig: German "talented; famous fighter"   Aug. 25

Luke: Latin "worshipful"   Oct. 18
    Lukas: Greek "light-hearted; creative"

Lullus   Oct. 16

Lupercus   Apr. 16

Luperius   Nov. 15

Lupicinus   Feb. 3

Luppus   Aug. 23

Lupus   July 29

Luxor   Aug. 21
    Luxorius

Lybosus   Dec. 29

M

Macarius	Jan. 2
Macaire	
Mace (Matthew): English "heavy staff or club"	Sept. 21
Macedon	Mar. 27
Macedonius	Mar. 13
Macniss	Sept. 3
Macrinus	Sept. 17
Macrobius	July 20
Macson (Maximus)	Aug. 13
Maden	May 17
Madern	
Maginus	Aug. 25
Maglorius	Oct. 24
Magnericus	July 25
Magnus: Latin "outstanding"	Jan. 1
Maieul	May 11
Mainard	Jan. 21
Maine	June 21
Major: Latin "leading"	May 10
Majorcus	Dec. 6
Malachy: Hebrew "angelic; magnanimous"	Jan. 14
Malchus	Mar. 28
Malcolm: Scottish "peaceful; devotee of Saint Columba"	June 3
Malo	Nov. 15
Mamas	Aug. 17
Mamilian	Mar. 12

Mamillus	Mar. 8
Mammertus	May 11
Mamertus	
Manahen	May 24
Manasses	Nov. 5
Mancius	May 15
Mandal: German "tough; almond"	June 10
Manetto	Aug. 20
Manfred: English "man of peace"	Jan. 28
Mansuetus	Feb. 19
Manuel: Hebrew, Spanish "gift from God; with us is God"	June 17
Mappalicus	Apr. 17
Maprilis	Aug. 22
Marcellian	June 18
Marcellin	Apr. 6
Marcellinus	Jan. 2
Marcellus: Latin "little warrior"	Jan. 16
Marcel: French "singing God's praises"	
Marcian	Jan. 4
Marcien	
Marcus	June 18
Mardarius	Dec. 13
Mardonius	Jan. 24
Mareas	Apr. 22
Marian	Jan. 17
Marianus	Aug. 19
Marinus	Mar. 3
Maris	Apr. 26

Marius: German "masculine; virile"   Jan. 19

Mark: Latin "combative, warring"   Apr. 25
    Marc: French "combative", **Marco**: Italian "tender", **Mario**: Italian "manly"

Marmaduke: English "haughty", Irish, Gaelic "follower of St. Maedoc"   Nov. 26

Marnack   Mar. 1

Marne   Sept. 2

Maro: Japanese "myself"   Apr. 15

Marolus   Apr. 23

Marotas   Mar. 27

Marshall: French "giving care; caretaker of horses"   June 30

Marten   Aug. 18

Martial: French "combative"   June 30

Martian   June 14

Martin: Latin "combative"   Nov. 11
    Marti, Martino, Martil, Mertin, Marvin: Welsh "sea friend"

Martinian   Jan. 2

Martinianus   Feb. 13

Martyrius   Jan. 23

Maruthas   Dec. 4
    Marutha

Mascula   Mar. 29
    Masculas

Maternus   July 18

Mathurin   Nov. 1
    Maturin

Matronian   Dec. 14

Matthew: Hebrew "God's gift"   Sept. 21
    Mathew, Mathies, Mathieu, Matt

Matthias: German "dignified; gift of God"　　　　　Feb. 24
　　Mathias

Maturus　　　　　June 2

Maur　　　　　Jan. 20

Maurice: Latin "dark"　　　　　Sept. 22
　　Maurus, Mauritz, Maury, Moris, Morris

Maurílius　　　　　Sept. 13

Maurinus　　　　　June 10
　　Maurin

Mauritius　　　　　July 10

Mavilus　　　　　Jan. 4

Maxentius　　　　　June 26

Maximian　　　　　Jan. 8

Maximilian: Latin "most wonderful"　　　　　Oct. 12
　　Max: Latin "best"

Maximin　　　　　June 8

Maximinus　　　　　May 29

Maximus　　　　　Jan. 8

Maynard: English "reliable", German "brave or hard strength"　　　　　May 9

Medard　　　　　June 8

Meinrad: Old German "strong or mighty counsel"　　　　　Jan. 21

Mel: English "friendly"　　　　　Feb. 6

Melanius　　　　　Jan. 6

Melas　　　　　Jan. 16

Melasippus　　　　　Nov. 7

Melchiades　　　　　Jan. 11

Melchior　　　　　Jan. 6

Meldan　　　　　Feb. 7

Meletius: Greek "very cautious"	Feb. 12
Meleusippus	Jan. 17
Mellitus	Apr. 24
Melvin: English "friendly"	July 17
Memmius	Aug. 5
Memnon	Aug. 20
Menalippus	Sept. 2
Menander	Apr. 28
Menedemus	Sept. 5
Meneleus	July 22
Meneus	July 24
Menignus	Mar. 15
Mennas	Aug. 25
Merald	Feb. 23
Merchard	Aug. 24
Mercurialis	May 23
Mercury: Latin "commerce"	Nov. 25
Merry	Aug. 29
Merulus	Jan. 17
Metellus	Jan. 24
Methodius: Greek "companion traveler"	July 7
Metran	Jan. 31
Metranus	
Metrobius	Dec. 24
Metrophanes	June 4
Meuris	Dec. 19
Michaeas	Jan. 15

Michael: Hebrew "who is like God?"   Sept. 29
    Micha: Hebrew "prophet", **Michal, Michaud, Michel**: French "fond", **Michele, Mickel, Miguel**: Spanish "who resembles God", **Mikel, Misha, Mitchell**: English "optimistic"

Migdonius   Dec. 23

Miles: German "forgiving"   Apr. 30
    Myles: English

Milles   Apr. 22

Milo: German "soft-hearted"   Feb. 23

Minercus   Aug. 23

Minervinus   Dec. 31

Minias   Oct. 25

Mirocles   Dec. 3

Miron   Aug. 8

Misael: Hebrew "godlike"   Dec. 16

Mitrius   Nov. 13

Modan   Feb. 4

Modestus   Jan. 12

Modoaldus   May 12
    Modoald

Monald   Mar. 15

Monas   Oct. 12

Monford   July 2

Monitor   Nov. 10

Montanus   Feb. 24

Moran   Oct. 22

Morand   June 3

More (St. Thomas)   July 9

Morgan: Welsh "circling sea"   May 15

Moritz   Nov. 2

Mortimer: French "deep; dead sea"   Aug. 12

Moses: Hebrew "drawn out of the water"   Sept. 4

Mosseus   Jan. 18

Mucian   July 3

Mucius   Apr. 22

Murdoch: Scottish "rich"   Sept. 2

Muritta   July 13

Musonius   Jan. 24

Myron: Greek "notable; myrrh, fragrant oil"   Aug. 8

N

Nabor	June 12
Nacaro	Jan. 8
Nahum	Dec. 1
Naldo (Ronald): Italian "smart tutor", Spanish "counselor-ruler"	Aug. 20
Namphanion	July 4
Napoleon: German "domineering"	Aug. 15
Napper (Bl. George)	Nov. 9
Narcissus: Greek "self-loving; vain"	Mar. 18
Narnus	Aug. 27
Narses	Mar. 27
Narseus	July 15
Narzales	July 17
Nathan: Hebrew "gift of God"	Dec. 29
Nathaniel: Hebrew "God's gift to mankind"	Aug. 24
Navalis	Dec. 16
Nazarius	July 28
Neal (Cornelius): Irish "winner"	Sept. 16
Neil: Irish, Gaelic "champion", **Nelson**: English "broad-minded"	
Ned (Edward): English "comforting; wealth protector"	Jan. 5
Nemesian	Sept. 10
Nemesius	Feb. 20
Nemesion	Dec. 19
Nemesius	Feb. 20
Nemorius	Sept. 7
Neon	Aug. 23
Neophytus	Jan. 20

Neopolus	May 2
Neoterius	Sept. 8
Nepomucene (St. John)	May 16
Nepomucen	
Nereus	May 12
Nersas	Nov. 20
Nestabus	Sept. 8
Nestor: Greek "wanderer; traveler"	Feb. 26
Neville (Alban): French "innovator; new village"	June 22
Nevin: Irish "small holy man; holy, sacred; little bone; servant of the saints's disciple"	
Nicaeas	June 22
Nicander	June 17
Nicanor	Jan. 10
Nicasius	Oct. 11
Nicephorus	Feb. 9
Nicetas	Jan. 7
Nicetius	Dec. 5
Nicetus	Apr. 2
Nicholas: Greek "winner; the people's victory"	Dec. 6
Nicolas: Italian "victorious", **Niles**: English "smooth; champion", **Niel, Nico**: Greek, Italian "victor"	
Nicodemus: Greek "people's victory"	Aug. 3
Nicomedes: Spanish, Greek "to ponder victory"	Sept. 15
Nicon	Mar. 23
Nicostratus	May 21
Nilammon	Jan. 6
Nilus	Feb. 20

Ninian: "studious"   Sept. 16
   Ninyas

Noah: Hebrew "peacemaker"   May 2
   Noe: Spanish "quiet"; Polish "comforter"

Noel: French: "Christmas"   Dec. 25

Nonnosus   Sept. 2

Nonnus   Dec. 2

Norbert: German "bright north"   June 6

Nostrian   Feb. 14

Novatus   June 20

Numerian   July 5

Numidicus   Aug. 9

O

Obert: German "bright and wealthy man"	Dec. 11
Oceanus	Sept. 4
Octavian: Latin "eight; able"	Mar. 22
Octavius	Nov. 20
Odemar	May 7
Odilo: Old German "fortunate or prosperous in battle"	Jan. 1
Odilon	Oct. 28
Odo: German "wealth"	Nov. 18
Odoric	Feb. 3
Olaf: Scandinavian "watchful", Old Norse "what remains of the ancestors"	July 29
Oleg: Russian "holy; religious"	Sept. 20
Oliver: Latin "loving nature; olive tree" **Olivier**: French "eloquent", **Olier**	July 11
Ollegar	Mar. 6
Olympias	Apr. 15
Olympius	June 12
Omer	Sept. 9
Onesimus	Feb. 16
Onesiphorus	Sept. 6
Onuphrius	June 12
Optatian	July 14
Optatus	June 4
Oran: Aramaic, Irish, Gaelic "light; pale" **Odran**	Oct. 27
Orentius	May 1
Orestes: Greek "mountain"	Dec. 13

Oriculus	Nov. 18
Orientius	May 1
Orlando: Spanish "famed; distinctive; renowned land" **Orland**	May 20
Ormond: Old English "kind-hearted; mountain of bears; spear or ship protector"	Jan. 23
Orontius	Jan. 22
Orson: Latin "strong as a bear"	Apr. 13
Oscar: Scandinavian "divine" **Oskar**	Feb. 3
Osee	July 4
Osmund: English "singing to the world" **Osmond**	Dec. 4
Ostian	June 30
Oswald: English "God's power"	Aug. 5
Othmar	Nov. 16
Otho	July 2
Otto: German "wealthy" **Othello**: Spanish "bold"	Jan. 16
Owen: Welsh "well-born; high-principled"	Aug. 24

P

Pachomius	May 9
Pacian: Spanish "peaceful"	Mar. 9
Pacificus	Sept. 24
Palaemon	Jan. 11
Palatinus	May 30
Palatius	Oct. 8
Palladius	July 6
Palmatius	May 10
Pambo	Sept. 6
Pammachius	Aug. 30
Pamphilus	June 1
Pancharius	Mar. 19
Pancho (Francis): Spanish "jaunty"	Oct. 4
Pancratius	Apr. 3
Pantaenus	July 7
Pantagapas	Sept. 2
Pantagathus	Apr. 17
Pantaleon: Spanish "pants; trousers; manly"	July 27
Papas	Mar. 16
Paphnutius	Apr. 19
Papias	Jan. 29
Papinian	Nov. 28
Papius	June 28
Papylus	Apr. 13
Paramon	Nov. 29

Paregorius	Feb. 18
Paris: English "lover"	Aug. 5
Parisius	June 11
Parmenas	Jan. 23
Parmenius	Apr. 22
Parthenius	May 19

Paschal: French "boy born on Easter; spiritual"
    Pascal: Latin "Easter child", **Pascoe, Pasquale**: Italian "spiritual",
    Pasinek
	May 17

Paschasius	Feb. 22
Pasicrates	May 25
Pastor: English "clergyman"	Mar. 29
Patapius	Dec. 8
Paterius	Feb. 21
Patermuthius	July 9
Paternian	July 12
Paternus	Apr. 16
Patience	May 1
Patiens	Jan. 8
Patrician	Oct. 10
Patricius	Apr. 28

Patrick: Irish "aristocrat; noble"
    Paton, Patrig, Patrizio, Payton, Peyton: Old English "fighting-
    man's estate"
	Mar. 17

Patrobas	Nov. 4
Patroclus	Jan. 21

Paul: Latin "small; wise"   Jan. 15
    Pablo: Spanish "strong; creative", **Paley, Paolo**: Italian "small and high energy", **Paulot, Paulus, Pavel**: Russian "inspired", **Pawel**: Polish "believer"

Paulillus   Dec. 19

Paulinus   June 22

Pausides   Mar. 24

Pausilippus   Apr. 15

Payne (Bl. John): Latin "countryman"   Apr. 2

Pegasius   Nov. 2

Peleus   Feb. 20

Peleusius   Apr. 7

Pelinus   Dec. 5

Pepin: German "ardent"   Feb. 21

Percy: French "mysterious"   Nov. 14
    Percival

Peregrine: Latin "traveler; wanderer"   May 1

Peregrinus   July 28

Perfectus   Apr. 18

Peronius   Sept. 6

Perpetuus   Apr. 8

Peter: Greek "dependable; rock"   Jan. 3
    Pearce, Peder, Pedro: Spanish "audacious", **Peirce, Pierce**: English "insightful; piercing", **Peire, Pierot, Perrin**: Latin "traveler", **Perry**: English "tough-minded; traveler, wanderer"

Petronius   Oct. 4

Pharnacius   June 24

Philadelphis   May 10

Philadelphus   Sept. 2

Philappian	Jan. 30
Philaeas	Feb. 4
Philastrius	July 18
Phileas	Nov. 26
Philemon: Greek "loving"	Mar. 8
Philibert	Aug. 20
Philip: Greek "outdoorsman; horse-lover"	May 1
Philo: Greek "love"	Apr. 25
Philogonius	Dec. 20
Philologus	Nov. 4
Philomenus	Nov. 14
Philoromus	Feb. 4
Philoterus	May 19
Philotheus	Nov. 5
Phineas: English "far-sighted"	Aug. 12
Phlegon	Apr. 8
Phocas	July 14
Photinus	June 2
Photius: Greek "scholarly"	Mar. 4
Piaton	Oct. 1
Pierius	Nov. 4
Pierson (Bl. Walter): English "rock"	May 4
Pigmenius	Mar. 24
Pinian	Dec. 31
Pinytus	Oct. 10
Pionius	Feb. 1
Piperion	Mar. 11

Pirmin	Nov. 3
Pius: Polish "pious"	May 5
Placidus: Latin "calm"	Oct. 5
Placid	
Plato: Greek "broad-minded; broad-shouldered"	Apr. 4
Platonides	Apr. 6
Plautus	Sept. 29
Plunket (Bl. Oliver)	July 11
Plutarch	June 28
Podius	May 28
Poemon	Aug. 27
Polius	May 21
Pollio	Apr. 28
Polyaenus	Apr. 28
Polyanus	Sept. 10
Polycarp	Jan. 26
Polychronius	Feb. 17
Polyeuctus	Feb. 13
Pompeius	July 7
Pompey	Dec. 14
Pompilio	July 15
Pomponius	Apr. 30
Pontian	Jan. 19
Ponticus	June 2
Pontius: Latin "the fifth"	Mar. 8
Poppo	Jan. 25
Porcarius	Aug. 12

Porphyrias	Nov. 4
Porphyry **Porphyrius**	Feb. 16
Porres (Bl. Martin)	Nov. 5
Portian	Nov. 24
Possidius	May 16
Potamon	May 18
Potentian	Dec. 31
Pothamius	Feb. 20
Potitus	Jan. 13
Praejectus	Jan. 25
Praesidius	Sept. 6
Praetextatus	Feb. 24
Pragmatius	Nov. 22
Priamus	May 28
Prilidian	Jan. 24
Primian	Dec. 29
Primitivus	Apr. 16
Primus	Jan. 3
Princeps	Aug. 22
Principius	Sept. 25
Priscian	Oct. 12
Priscillian	Jan. 4
Priscus	Jan. 4
Privatus	Aug. 21
Probus	Jan. 12
Processus	July 2

Prochorus	Apr. 9
Proclus	Oct. 24
Procopius	Feb. 27
Proculus	Feb. 14
Projectus	Jan. 24
Prosdocimus	Nov. 7
Prosper: Italian "having good fortune"	June 25
Protase	June 19
Protasius	
Protogenes	May 6
Protolicus	Feb. 14
Protus	Sept. 11
Prudentius	Apr. 28
Ptolemy	Aug. 24
Publius	Jan. 21
Pudens	May 19
Pupulus	Feb. 28
Pusicius	Apr. 21

Q

Quadragesimus	Oct. 26
Quadratus	Mar. 26
Quartan	Sept. 3
Quartus	May 10
Quentin: Latin "fifth"	Oct. 31
Quillen (William)	Jan. 10
Quinctian	Apr. 1
Quinctilian	Apr. 13
Quinctilis	Mar. 8
Quinctus	Jan. 4
Quinidius	Feb. 15
Quintian	Nov. 13
Quintin	Oct. 31
Quiriacus	Aug. 23
Quiricus	June 16
Quirin: English "a magic spell"	June 4
Quirinus: Latin "spear"	Oct. 11
Quodvultdeus	Feb. 19

R

Rainald	Aug. 18
Rainer: German "advisor; deciding warrior"	Dec. 30
Rainier	
Rainerius	June 17
Ralph: English "advisor to all; wolf counsel"	May 27

    Randal: English "secretive", **Randall**: Old German "wolf shield", **Randolph**: English "protective", German "wolf shield", **Randolf**, **Raoul**: Spanish "confidant; wolf counsel", **Rolf**: German "famous wolf; kind advisor", **Rollo**: German "famous", **Roul**, **Rodolfo**: Spanish "spark", Old German "famous wolf"

Rambert: German "pleasant kid"	June 13
Randaut	Feb. 21
Randoald	
Raphael: Hebrew "God has healed"	Oct. 24
Rasyphus	July 23
Raymond: English "strong", Old German "protecting hands"	Jan. 6
Raimundo, Ramon: Spanish "protecting hands"	
Raymund	Aug. 26
Raynald	Aug. 18
Rayner: French "counselor"	Feb. 22
Raynier	
Reatrus	Jan. 27
Redemptus	Apr. 8
Reginald: English "wise advisor", Latin "ruler's advisor"	Apr. 9
Reynold: English "knowledgeable tutor", **Reinald**: French "judges", **Reynaud**: French "advisor", **Reynalt**	
Regius	June 18
Regnier	Feb. 22
Regulus	Mar. 30

Reinhard	Mar. 7
Reinhold (Reginald)	Sept. 17
Reinold	Jan. 7
Rembert	Feb. 4
Remedius	Feb. 3
Remi: French "fun-loving"	Oct. 1
Remigius	Oct. 1
Remy: French "from Rheims"	Jan. 13
Rene: French "born again" **Renier, Reno**: Spanish	Feb. 22
Respicius	Nov. 10
Restitutus	May 29
Reverian	June 1
Revocatus	Jan. 9
Rex: Latin "king"	Apr. 9
Rhais	June 28
Rhenus	Feb. 24
Rhodian	Mar. 20
Rich (Bl. Edmund): English "affluent"	Nov. 16
Richard: English "wealthy leader", Old German "powerful leader" **Ricardo**: Spanish "snappy", **Ritch**: American "leader", **Ritchie, Rykart**	Feb. 7
Richarius	Apr. 26
Rigobertus: "strong" **Rigobert**	Jan. 4
Robert: English "brilliant; renowned" **Robard, Roberto**: Spanish "bright and famous", **Robin**: English "gregarious"	May 13
Robustian	May 24

Roch   Aug. 16
    Rock, Roque

Rochester (Bl. John): Old English "stone camp or fortress"   May 4

Rodan   Apr. 15

Roderic   May 13
    Roderick: German "effective leader; famous power", **Roderigo, Royce**: English "affluent", **Ruy**

Rodion   Apr. 8

Rodolf   July 27

Rodopian   May 3

Rogatian   May 24

Rogatus   Jan. 12

Rogellus   Sept. 16

Roger: German "famed warrior; renowned spearman"   Aug. 16
    Rogerio, Rogero, Rodger, Rutger, Rory: Irish, Gaelic "red", German "strong", **Rorie**

Roland: German "renowned land"   Nov. 15
    Rolando: Spanish "famous", **Rowland**: Scandinavian "famous"

Romain   Feb. 28
    Roman: Latin "citizen of Rome; fun-loving"

Romanus   Feb. 28

Romaricus   Dec. 8

Romeo: Latin "citizen of Rome", Italian "romantic lover"   Mar. 4

Romuald   Feb. 7

Romulus: Latin "man of Rome; presumptuous"   Feb. 17

Ronald: English "helpful", Old Norse "ruler's counselor"   Aug. 20

Ronan: Irish "seal; playful"   June 1

Rothard   Oct. 14

Ruben: Spanish "see, a son"   Aug. 4

Rubert	May 15
Ruderic	Mar. 13
Rudolph: German "famous wolf"	July 27
Rudolf, Rudolphe, Rolph, Rollin	
Ruffillus	July 18
Rufinian	Sept. 9
Rufinus	Feb. 28
Rufus: Latin "redhead"	Nov. 21
Roy: French "king"	
Rumold	July 1
Rupert: English "prince"	Mar. 27
Ruprecht	
Rurik: Russian "famous power"	May 13
Rusticus	Aug. 9
Rutilius	Aug. 2
Rutilus	June 4
Rutulus	Feb. 18

S

Sabas	Apr. 12
Sabbas	Dec. 5
Sabbatius	Sept. 19
Sabel	June 17
Sabellus	Jan. 29
Sabinian	Jan. 29
Sabinianus	June 7
Sabinus	Jan. 25
Sacerdos	May 4

Sacha (Alexander): Russian "defends; man's defender; charms"   Feb. 26
    Sanders: English "kind; son of Alexander", **Sandy**: English "personable"

Sadoth	Feb. 20
Sagar	Oct. 6
Sallustian	June 8
Salutaris	July 13

Salvatore: Italian "rescuer; spirited"   Mar. 18

Salvinus	Oct. 12
Salvius	Jan. 11
Samonas	Nov. 15

Sampson: Hebrew "strong man"   July 28
    Samson: Hebrew "son"

Samuel: Hebrew "man who heard God; prophet"   Feb. 16
    Samuele

Sancho: Latin "genuine; sacred"   June 5

Sanctinus	Sept. 22

Sanctus: Latin "holy"   June 2
  Sanctos

Sandal   Sept. 3

Sandor (Alexander): Greek "savior of mankind; nice", Hungarian   Jan. 11
  "man's defender"
  Sandro

Santiago (St. James): Spanish "sainted; valuable"   July 25

Sarmata   Oct. 11

Saturnian   Oct. 16

Saturninus   Jan. 19

Saturus   Mar. 29

Satyrus   Jan. 12

Saul: Hebrew "gift; prayed for"   Feb. 16

Savero (Xavier): "renewal"   Dec. 3

Savinus   July 11

Scillitan   July 17

Scubiculus   Oct. 11

Sebald   Aug. 19

Sebastian: Latin "dramatic; honorable", Greek "revered"   Jan. 20

Sebbe   Aug. 29

Secundarius   Oct. 2

Secundian   Feb. 17

Secundinus   Feb. 18

Secundulus   Mar. 7

Secundus   Jan. 9

Securus   Dec. 2

Selesius   Sept. 12

Seleucus   Feb. 16

Senator	Sept. 26
Sennen: English "aged"	July 30
Septiminus	Sept. 1
Septimus: Latin "seventh"	Aug. 17
Sequanus	Sept. 19
Seraphinus	Oct. 12
Serapion	Mar. 21
Seran	Mar. 6
Serenus	June 28
Sergius	Sept. 8
Serge, Sergio: Italian "handsome", Latin "servant; attendant"	
Servandus	Oct. 23
Servatius	May 13
Servideus	Jan. 13
Servilian	Apr. 20
Servilius	May 24
Servulus	Feb. 21
Servus	Dec. 7
Servusdeus	Sept. 16
Seth: Hebrew "chosen"	Mar. 1
Severian	Jan. 23
Severin: Latin "severe; stern"	Jan. 8
Severus	Jan. 11
Seward (Siviard): English "guarding the sea; victory guardian"	Mar. 1
Sextus: Latin "sixth child; mischievous"	Dec. 31
Shamus (James): Irish "seizing"	July 25
Shawn (John): English "grace in God"	Dec. 27

Sheil   Feb. 12

Sherwin (Bl. Ralph): English "fleet of foot; bright friend"   Dec. 1

Sherwood (Bl. Thomas): English "bright options; luminous wood"   Mar. 7

Sibold   Oct. 26

Sidney: French "attractive", Old English "wide meadow"   Sept. 19

Sidonius   Aug. 21

Sidronius   July 11

Sigefried: German "victor"   Feb. 15
> **Sigefrid, Sigefride**

Sigfrid   Feb. 15
> **Siward**

Sigismund   May 1
> **Sigmund**: German "winner; victorious hand or protector"

Silas: Latin "saver; forest, woods"   July 13

Silvanus: Latin "woods"   Feb. 6

Silverius   June 20

Silvester: Latin "wooded"   Dec. 31

Silvinus   Feb. 17

Silvio   May 31
> **Sylvio**

Silvius   Apr. 21

Simeon: Hebrew "to hear, to be heard; reputation"   Feb. 18

Similian   June 16

Simitrius   May 26

Simon: Hebrew "good listener; thoughtful"   Oct. 28
> **Simone**

Simplician   Aug. 16

Simplicius   Mar. 10

Sinclair (St. Claire): French "prayerful"	Nov. 4
Sindimius	Dec. 19
Sindulph	Dec. 10
Sindulphus	Oct. 20
Sirenus	Feb. 23
Siricius	Feb. 21
Siridion	Jan. 2
Sirmion	Apr. 9
Sisenand	July 16
Sisinius	May 11
Siviard	Mar. 1
Sixtus: Latin "sixth child"	Apr. 3
Slade (Bl. Thomas): English "quiet child; valley"	Oct. 30
Smaragdus	Aug. 8
Sobel	Aug. 5
Socrates: Greek "philosophical; brilliant"	Apr. 19
Solemnius	Sept. 25
Solochan	May 17
Solomon: Hebrew "peaceful and wise"	Mar. 13
Solutor	Nov. 20
Sophonias	Dec. 3
Sophronius	Mar. 11
Sosipater	June 25
Sosius	Sept. 19
Sosteneo	May 3
Sosthenes	Sept. 10
Soter	Apr. 22

Sozon	Sept. 7
Speciosus	Mar. 15
Speratus	July 17
Spes	Mar. 28
Speusippus	Jan. 17
Spiridion: Greek "like a breath of fresh air"	Dec. 14
Spur	Jan. 16
Stachis	Oct. 31
Stacteus	July 18
Stanislaus: Latin "glorious"	Aug. 15
Stanislao, Stanko, Stanley: English "stony meadow; traveler"	
Stephen: Greek "victorious; crown, garland"	Feb. 8
Stephan, Stefano: Italian "supreme ruler", **Stepka, Steven**	
Stercatius	July 24
Strato	Sept. 9
Straton	Aug. 17
Stratonicus	Jan. 13
Sturmius	Dec. 17
Stylian	Nov. 26
Styriacus	Nov. 2
Successus	Jan. 19
Sulpice	Jan. 17
Sulpicius	Jan. 29
Superius	June 26
Suranus	Jan. 24
Swidbert	Mar. 1
Swithin: English "swift, strong"	July 2
Swithum	

Syagrius	Aug. 27
Sycus	May 30
Sydney: English	Dec. 10
Sylvanus	Feb. 18
Sylvester: Latin "forest dweller; heavy-duty"	Dec. 31
Symmachus	July 19
Symphorian	July 7
Symphronius	Feb. 3
Synesius	May 21
Syntyche	July 22
Syrius	June 29
Syrus	Dec. 9

T

Tammarius	Sept. 1
Tancred: Old German "well-considered counsel or advice"	Apr. 9
Tarachus	Oct. 11
Tarasius	Feb. 25
Tarcissus	Aug. 15
Tatian **Tation**	Aug. 24
Taurio	Nov. 7
Tedmund (Edmund): Old English "protector of the land"	Nov. 16
Tegan: Irish	Sept. 9
Telesphorus: Greek "leading to an end; centered"	Jan. 5
Terence: Irish "tender" **Terrence, Terry**: Old German "power of the tribe"	June 21
Terentian	Sept. 1
Tertius	Dec. 6
Tertullian	Apr. 27
Tertullinus	Aug. 4
Thaddeus: Greek "courageous", Aramaic "heart"	Oct. 28
Thalalaeus	May 20
Thalus	Mar. 11
Thamel	Sept. 4
Tharacus	Oct. 11
Tharasius	Feb. 25
Tharsicius	Jan. 31
Thaurinus	Aug. 11
Themistocles	Dec. 21

Theobald: German "brave man"	June 30
Theodard	Sept. 10
Theodemir	July 25
Theodore: Greek "God's gift; a blessing"	Jan. 7
Theodor	
Theodoric: Old German "God's gift; power of the tribe"	July 1
Theodric, Thierry	
Theodosius	Jan. 11
Theodotus	May 6
Theodulphus	June 24
Theodulus	Feb. 17
Theogenes	Jan. 3
Theogonius	Aug. 21
Theonas	Jan. 3
Theonestus	Oct. 30
Theopemptus	Jan. 3
Theophanes	Mar. 12
Theophilus: Greek "loved by God"	Jan. 8
Theopistus	Sept. 20
Theopompus	May 21
Theoprepides	Mar. 27
Theoticus	Mar. 8
Theotimus	Apr. 20
Thespesius	June 1
Theusetas	Mar. 13
Thibaud	June 30
Thomais	Apr. 14

Thomas: Greek "twin; lookalike"   Dec. 21
    Tomas, Tomasso, Tomaz

Thraseas   Oct. 5

Thrason   Dec. 11

Thurstan   Mar. 31

Thyrsus   Jan. 24

Tiberius   Nov. 10

Tiburtius   Apr. 14

Tigides   Feb. 3

Timolaus   Mar. 24

Timon: Greek "respect"   Apr. 19

Timothy: Greek "reveres God; God's honor"   Jan. 24

Titian   Jan. 16

Titus: Latin "heroic; defender"   Jan. 4
    Tito: Latin "honored"

Tobias: Hebrew "the Lord is good"   Nov. 2

Torpes   Apr. 29

Torquatus   May 15

Totnan   July 8

Toussaint (All Saints): French "all saints"   Nov. 1
    Toussant

Trajan   Dec. 23

Tranquillinus   July 6

Triphenes   Jan. 31

Triphyllius   June 13

Tripos   June 10

Troadius   Dec. 28

Trojan   Nov. 30

Trophimus	Mar. 11
Trudo	Nov. 23
Trypho	July 3
Tryphon	Jan. 4
Turian	July 13
Turibius	Mar. 23
Tybalt: Greek "always right"	June 30
Tychicus	Apr. 29
Tychon: Greek "accurate"	June 16
Tyrannio	Feb. 20

U

Ubaldus	May 16
Ugo (Hugh): Italian "bright mind; a thinker"	Apr. 29
Ugoccio	May 3
Ugolino	Oct. 10
Uldaric	July 4
Ulric: English, Old German "power of the wolf; power of the home"	
Ulmer: Old English "fame of the wolf"	July 20
Urban: Latin "city dweller"	July 29
Urbanus	Jan. 24
Ursicinus	June 19
Ursicius	Aug. 14
Ursinus	Nov. 9
Ursino	
Ursiscenus	June 21
Ursmar	Apr. 19
Ursus	Apr. 13
Usthazanes	Apr. 21

V

Valens	May 21
Valentine: Latin "robust, healthy"	Feb. 14
Valentio	May 25
Valerian: Russian, Latin "strong leader; healthy"	Apr. 14
Valerius	Jan. 28
Valery	Apr. 1
Valter (Walter)	June 4
Vardan	Aug. 7
Varicus	Nov. 15
Varus	Oct. 19
Vedast	Feb. 6
Venantius	Apr. 1
Venerand	May 25
Venerandus	Nov. 14
Venerius	May 4
Venturius	July 17
Venustian	Dec. 30
Venustus	May 6
Veranus	Oct. 19
Verecundius	Oct. 22
Verian	Aug. 9
Veríssimus	Oct. 1
Vernon (Berno): Latin "fresh and bright", Old French "alder grove"	Jan. 13
Verulus	Feb. 21
Verus	Aug. 1

Vetius	June 2
Viator: Latin "voyager through life"	Oct. 21
Victor: Latin "victorious; champion"	Jan. 22
Victorian	Mar. 23
Victoricus	Feb. 24
Victorinus	Feb. 25
Victorius	Oct. 30
Victricius	Aug. 7
Victurus	Dec. 18
Vigilius	June 26
Vigor	Nov. 1
Vinard	Oct. 11
Vincent: Latin "victorious; prevailing" **Vicente, Vincens, Vincenti, Vance**: Old English "marshland"	Jan. 22
Vindemial	May 2
Virgil: Latin "holding his own; writer"	Nov. 27
Vitalian	Jan. 27
Vitalicus	Sept. 4
Vitalis: Latin "bubbly; vital"	Jan. 9
Vitus: Latin "winning"	June 15
Viventiolus	July 12
Viventius	Jan. 13
Vivian: Latin "full of life" **Vivien**	Aug. 28
Vladimar: Russian "glorious leader"	July 15
Volusian	Jan. 18
Vulpian	Apr. 3

W

Wallabonsus	June 7
Walstan	May 30
Walter: German "army leader"	June 4
Walther, Walthier, Water, Wolter	
Wandrille	July 22
Ward (Bl. William): Old English "watchman"	July 26
Warren: German "safe haven", English "park warden; watchman"	Feb. 6
Webster (Bl. Augustine): English "creative; weaver"	Feb. 6
Wenceslaus: Polish "glorified king", Slavic "greater glory"	Sept. 28
Wenzel, Wenceslas	
Wendelyn	Oct. 21
Wendel, Wendell: German "full of wanderlust"	
Werner: German "warrior; army defender"	Apr. 19
Wigbert	Aug. 13
Wilbert: German "smart; bright will"	Sept. 11
Wilbur: English "fortified"	
Wilfrid: German "peacemaker"	Oct. 12
Wilfred: Old English "desiring peace"	
Willehad	Nov. 8
William: English "staunch protector", German "will helmet, protection"	Jan. 10
Wilhelm: German "resolute; determined", **Willin**	
Willibald	July 7
Willibrord	Nov. 7
Winfred	Nov. 3
Winfrid	
Winoc	Nov. 6
Winwaloe	Mar. 3

Wiro	May 8
Wistremund	June 7
Wolfgang: German "talented; a wolf walks" **Wolf**	Oct. 31
Wright (Bl. Peter): English "clear-minded; correct; carpenter"	May 19
Wulfram **Wulfran**	Mar. 20
Wulmar	July 20
Wulstan	Jan. 19

X

Xavier (St. Francis): Arabic "shining", Spanish "bright; splendid; new house"   Dec. 3
    Xaver, Xavery

Ximen (Simon): Spanish "obeys"   Oct. 28

Xistus (Sixtus)   Apr. 6

Y

Yago (James)   July 25

Yves: French "honest; handsome; archer's bow"   May 19
    Yvo

Z

Zachaeus	Aug. 23
Zacharas	May 26
Zachary: Hebrew "spiritual; the Lord recalled"	Nov. 5
Zacharius: Hebrew "devout"	
Zamas	Jan. 24
Zambdas	Feb. 19
Zanitas	Mar. 27
Zenas: Greek "powerful; hospitable"	June 23
Zeno: Greek "philosophical; stoic"	Feb. 14
Zenobius: "lively"	Feb. 20
Zephyrinus	Aug. 26
Zeticus	Dec. 23
Zoellus	May 24
Zoilus	June 27
Zosimus	Jan. 3
Zoticus	Jan. 12

Girls

A

Acacia: Greek "thorny, pointy; everlasting; tree"   Mar. 29
    Acatia

Acra   June 8

Ada: German "noble, kind; joyful"   Dec. 4
    Adna, Adonetta

Adamina (Adam): Hebrew "the earth; red earth; earth child"   Dec. 24

Adavisa   Aug. 29

Adelaide: German "noble, kind; calming; distinguished"   Dec. 16
    Addie, Adelais, Adelecia, Adleta

Adelina: German "noble"   Oct. 20
    Adelia, Adeline: English "sweet", German "noble"

Adela: German "noble", Polish "peacemaker"   Feb. 24
    Adel: Hebrew, German "God is eternal; noble, highborn", **Adella,**
    Adele: "giving", **Adeliza**

Adilia   Dec. 13

Adolphina   June 17
    Adolphine

Adria: Greek "dark, rich"   Dec. 2
    Adrianne

Adriana: Greek, Latin "dark, rich; exotic"   Aug. 10

Aemilia (Emilian)   Sept. 11

Aemiliana   June 30

Aerenia   Mar. 8

Afra: Hebrew, Arabic "whitish red; deer; lithe; color of the earth"   May 24

Afrina   Oct. 21

Agapa   Aug. 8

Agape: Greek "love"   Feb. 15

Agapes   Dec. 28

Agatha: Greek "good; kind-hearted; honorable"   Feb. 5
    Agata, Agathe, Aggie

Agathadorus   Apr. 13

Agathoclia   Sept. 17

Agathonica   Apr. 13

Agnes: Greek "chaste; pure, holy", Latin "lamb"   Jan. 21
    Agna, Agne, Agneda, Agnella, Agnessa, Agnese, Agneta

Agrippina   June 23

Aileen (Helen); Irish, Scottish "fair-haired beauty"   Aug. 18

Aimee: French "beloved"   June 10
    Aime

Alacoque (St. Margaret Mary)   Oct. 17

Alane   Nov. 25
    Alanna: "pretty girl"

Alaranna   Nov. 26

Alba: Latin, Italian, Spanish "dawn; white"   Jan. 17

Alberta: German "bright nobility", French "bright-eyed"   Mar. 11
    Albertina: Portuguese "bright", **Albertine**: English "bright",
    Albrette

Albina: Latin "white, bright"   Dec. 16

Alcidia   May 29

Alda: German "noble; the older child; old, prosperous"   Apr. 26

Aldegund   Jan. 30

Alena: Hebrew "tower"   June 24

Alexandra: Greek "to defend, help; regal protector   May 18
    Alesandra, Alexandrina, Alexandrine: French "helpful", **Alexa**:
    Greek, **Alexine**

Alexia: Greek "to defend, help; bright"   June 29
    Alexis: Greek "helpful; pretty; defender, protector"

Alfonsa: German "noble and ready"   Aug. 2
    Alphonsina, Alonsa: Old German "ready for battle"

Alfreda: Old English "elf and counsel; wise advisor"   Aug. 2

Alfrida   Dec. 8

Alice (Adelaide): Greek "honest", Old German "noble, exalted nature"   Dec. 16
    Alicia: Greek "delicate; lovely", Old German "noble, exalted nature",
    Aline: Polish "noble family", **Alexie, Alisa**: Hebrew "great happiness",
    Allis, Alyce, Alletta, Alyssa: Greek "flourishing; rational"

Alma (A title of Our Blessed Mother): Latin, Italian, Hebrew, Aramic
    "good; soulful; nourshing, kind; young woman; learned"

Alodia   Oct. 22

Aloysia   Sept. 12
    Aloys, Aloisia: Old German "famous warrior", **Aloyza**

Alva: Hebrew "highness", Spanish "fair; bright"   Sept. 11

Alverna: English "truthful friend"   Sept. 14
    Alvernia

Alvina: English "beloved; friendly; elf or supernatural being"   June 2

Alvira   Mar. 6

Amabilis   Nov. 1
    Amabel: Latin "lovable, amiable", **Amabelle**: American "loved"

Amanda: Latin, English, Irish "lovable; loved"   June 18

Amarna   July 8

Amata	June 10
Ambrosine (Ambrose): Greek "immortal; everlasting"	Dec. 7
Amelberga	July 10
Amelia: Latin, Old German "industrious, striving; work" **Amelie**	June 2
America (Emmeric)	Nov. 4
Ammia	Aug. 31
Ammonaria	Dec. 12
Amy (Amata): Latin, Old French "loved one" **Amicia**	June 10
Anastasia: Greek, Russian "reborn; royal; resurrection"	Dec. 25
Anatolia: Greek "break of day" **Anatola**: Greek, French "dawn"	July 9
Andrea (Andrew): Greek "feminine" **Andrene**	Nov. 30
Androna	Nov. 3
Angela: Greek "divine; angelic; messenger of God" **Ancela, Angele, Angelique, Angelita, Anjela, Aniela**	May 31
Angelina: Latin "angelic"	July 15
Anicia	May 11
Anna: English, Italian, German, Russian, Polish "gracious"	Sept. 1
Anne: English "generous" **Anita**: Spanish "gracious", **Anitra, Annabel, Annabelle**: English "lovely girl", **Annata, Annie, Anusia**	July 26
Annunciata (*for the Annunciation of Our Blessed Mother*): Italian "noticed, announcement"	Mar. 25
Anselina **Anselma**: Old German "helmet of God"	Apr. 21
Anthia	Apr. 18
Anthusa	July 27

Antigone (Antigonus)	Feb. 27
Antoinette: French, Latin "quintessential"	May 3
Antoinetta, Antonetta: Greek "praised"	
Antonia: Latin "perfect"	Apr. 29
Antonina	May 3
Anysia	Dec. 30
Anisia, Annice	
Apollonia: Greek	Feb. 9
Aquila	Jan. 23
Aquilina: Latin "eagle"	June 13
Arabia	Mar. 13
Archangela	Feb. 13
Ardalia	Apr. 14
Ariadne: Greek "holiness; most holy"	Sept. 17
Ariadna	
Arilda	Oct. 30
Armella	Oct. 24
Arnoldine	Mar. 14
Asella	Dec. 6
Asteria: "star-like"	Aug. 10
Athanasia: Greek "eternal life"	Aug. 14
Attracta	Aug. 11
Auberta (Albert): French	Nov. 15
Audrey: Old English "strong and regal"	June 23
Audry, Aubrie: French, German "noble being"	
Augusta: Latin "revered, great, magnificent"	Mar. 27
Asta: Greek, Old Norse "star-like; love"	
Aulaire	Feb. 12

Aura: Greek "breeze; wind"   July 19

Aurea   Aug. 24

Aurelia: Latin "golden"   Dec. 2

Austine: Latin "respected, great, magnificent"   Aug. 28

Austreberta   Feb. 10

Ava: Latin "pretty; delicate bird"   Apr. 29

Aveline (Eve)   Dec. 19

Avida   May 7

Avoice (Hedwig)   Oct. 16

Azelle   Dec. 6

B

Babette (Elizabeth): French "little Barbara; foreign" Nov. 5

Babilla May 20

Balbina: Latin "little stutterer" Mar. 31

Baptista: Latin "one who baptizes" June 24

Barbara: Greek, Latin "unusual stranger; foreign woman" Dec. 4
Barba, Barbe, Barica, Barbora

Barbea Jan. 29

Bartillia Jan. 3

Basila Aug. 29

Basilia: Greek "regal; royal" Mar. 13

Basilica Nov. 29

Basilissa Jan. 9

Basilla May 17

Bassa Mar. 6

Bathilde: German "woman who wars" Jan. 30
Baldechilde, Bathildes

Beata: German, Latin "blessed" Mar. 8

Beatrice: Latin "blessed woman, voyager through life; joyful" July 29
Bea, Beatrix: Latin "happy"

Begga Dec. 17

Belina Feb. 19
Belinda: Latin, Spanish "beautiful serpent"

Belle (Isabel): French "beautiful" July 8
Belita

Bellina: French "beautiful" Sept. 9

Benedicta: Latin "woman blessed"   Jan. 4
    Benedeta, Beneta, Benita: Latin, Spanish "lovely", **Benite, Benoite,**
    Benedetta: Latin "blessed"

Benilda   June 15

Berenice: Greek "victory bringer"   Oct. 4
    Bernice: Greek "victorious"

Berina   Nov. 26

Bernadette: French, Old German "strong, brave bear; brave"   Apr. 16

Bernarda   May 20
    Bernadina, Bernardine: German "brave"

Bertha: German "bright, famous"   July 4
    Berthel, Bertel

Bertilla   Jan. 3
    Bertilia, Bertina: German "bright, shining"

Bertille: German "bright maiden"   Nov. 5

Bess (Elizabeth)   Nov. 5
    Beta: Greek "beginning", **Betha:** Welsh "devoted to God", **Betina,**
    Betsey, Betta, Bettina: Hebrew "God's promise", **Betty:** Hebrew
    "God's promise; God-loving"

Beth: Hebrew "house"   Dec. 5

Betilda   Jan. 26

Beverley: English "friendly; beaver stream"   May 7
    Beverly: Old English "beaver stream or meadow"

Bibiana: Spanish "alive"   Dec. 2

Birona   Mar. 8

Blanche: French, Old German "pure; white"   July 5
    Bianca: Italian "pure; white", **Branca, Blanca:** Spanish "white",
    Blanch

Blanda: Latin "seductive; amiable"   May 10

Blandina   June 2
    Blandine

Bobilia   Oct. 16

Bona: Latin, Polish, Italian, Spanish "good"   Apr. 24

Bonnie: English, Scottish "fine, attractive, pretty"   May 29

Bonosa   July 15

Brenda (Brendan): Irish "royal; glowing", Old Norse "sword"   May 16

Briana (Brian): Irish "virtuous; strong"   Mar. 22

Bridget: Irish "powerful", Gaelic "exalted one"   Feb. 1
    Bridgit, Bride, Brigette, Brigid, Brigitta: Romanian "strong",
    Bristta, Brita

Burga (Walburga)   Feb. 25

Burgundofara   Apr. 3

Buriana   June 4

C

Calista: Latin, Greek "most beautiful; fairest"	Sept. 2
Calliopa	June 8
Callinica	Mar. 22
Callista: Geek "most beautiful"	Apr. 25
Camelia **Camella**	Sept. 16
Camilla: Italian, Latin "wonderful" **Camila, Camille**: French "swift runner; great innocence"	Mar. 3
Candia	Oct. 22
Candida: Latin "white"	June 6
Canice	Oct. 11
Cantianilla	May 31
Capitolina	Oct. 27
Careme	Sept. 7
Carina: Greek, Italian "dearest", Latin "beloved"	Nov. 7
Carisia	May 6
Carissima	Sept. 7
Carita: Latin "giving; loved"	June 12
Carmel (*Our Lady of Mount Carmel*): Hebrew "garden, orchard" **Carmela**: Hebrew, Italian "fruitful", **Carmelita, Carmen**: Hebrew "crimson", Latin, Spanish "song"	July 16
Carmilla	Mar. 23

Caroline (Charles): German "petite woman"   Nov. 4
    Carla: Latin, **Carlen**: "winner", **Carleen**: "sweet", **Carletta**: "affectionate", **Carlina, Carlinna, Carlin**: Gaelic "little champion", Latin, German "winner", **Carlita**: Italian "outstanding", **Carilla, Carol**: English "feminine", French "joyful song", German "farming woman", **Carolina**: Italian "feminine", **Carrie**: French, English "joyful song", **Charlene**: French "petite and beautiful", **Charlet, Cheryl**: French "beloved"

Casdoa   Sept. 29

Casilda: Latin "from the dwelling"   Apr. 9

Cassandra (Alexandra): Greek "insightful; unheeded prophetess"   May 18

Cassia: Greek "spicy; cinnamon"   July 20

Cassilda   Apr. 9

Catalina: Spanish "pure"   May 11

Catherine (Catherine): Greek, Irish, English "pure"   Apr. 30
    Catharine, Catana, Catania, Caterina, Cathleen: Irish "pure; immaculate"

Cazaria   Dec. 8

Cecilia: Latin, Polish "blind; short-sighted"   Nov. 22
    Caecilia, Cecile: Latin "gentile", **Cecily, Celia**: Latin, **Celie, Celine**: Greek "lovely", **Cicile, Cisily**: "clever"

Celerina   Feb. 3

Celeste: Latin "gentle and heavenly"   Apr. 16
    Celesta

Celestina: "heavenly"   May 10

Cella (Marcella)   Jan. 31

Centolla   Aug. 13

Cera: French "colorful"   Jan. 5

Cerenna   Nov. 15

Charitina   Oct. 5

Charity: Latin "loving; affectionate; dear"   Aug. 1
    Charissa: Greek "giving", **Cherry**: Latin, French "cherry red"

Charlotte (Charles): French "little woman"   Nov. 4
    Carlota, Carlotta: Italian, Spanish "sweetheart", **Charlet**

Charmaine (Charlemagne): Latin "womanly", French "singer"   Jan. 28

Chelidonia   Oct. 13

Chiara: Italian "bright and clear"   Jan. 5

Chionia   Apr. 3

Christeta   Oct. 27

Christiana: Greek, German "Christ's follower"   Dec. 15

Christina: Greek, Scottish, German, Irish "the anointed one; Christian"   July 24
    Christa: German, Greek "loving", **Christabel**: Latin, French
    "beautiful Christian", **Christabelle, Christal**: Latin, **Christel,**
    Christine: French, English, Latin "faithful", **Cristina, Crystal**:
    Latin "clear; open-minded", Greek "ice"

Chrysa   Aug. 24

Cilinia   Oct. 21

Cineria   Oct. 29

Cinthia   Feb. 8

Clara: Latin "bright one; famous, brilliant"   Aug. 12
    Claire: Latin, French "smart; famous", **Clare, Clareta**: Spanish
    "bright", **Clarice**: Latin, Italian "insightful; fame", **Clarinda**: Latin
    "bright", **Clarine, Claribel**: English "bright; beautiful", **Claribelle**:
    "bright lovely woman", **Clarissa**: Latin, Greek "smart and clear-
    minded", **Clarita, Chiara**: Italian "bright and clear; light"

Claudia: Latin "lame", German, Italian "persevering"   May 18
    Claudina, Claudine, Claudette: French "persistent"

Clementina: Spanish "kind; forgiving"   June 5
    Clemency, Clementine: Latin, French "merciful"

Cleopatra: Greek "father's glory"   Oct. 19
    Cleo

Clotilde: French "combative" June 3
    Clotilda: German "famed fighter; renowned battle", **Clotildis**

Cointha Feb. 8

Colette: French "spiritual; victorious; people of victory" Mar. 6
    Coletta, Collette

Colona Dec. 31

Columba: Latin "dove" Sept. 17

Columbina May 22
    Columbine: Latin "dove; flower"

Comelia Apr. 20

Conception (*The Immaculate Conception*): Spanish "conceived; begins" Dec. 8
    Concha, Conchita: Spanish "girl of the conception", **Concetta**: Italian

Concessa Apr. 8

Concordia: Latin "peace, harmony" Aug. 13

Condita Aug. 14

Conradine: Old German "brave counsel" Nov. 26

Consortia June 22

Constance: Latin "loyal; constancy; steadfastness" Sept. 19
    Connie: Latin, French "constant", **Constancia, Constantia**

Consuelo (*Our Lady of Consolation*): Latin, Old French, Spanish "comfort-giver; consolation"
    Consuela, Consolata

Cordula: Latin "heart", German "jewel" Oct. 22
    Cordelia: Latin "warm-hearted woman", **Cora**: Greek "maid; giving girl", **Corinne**: Greek "maiden", French "protective"

Corintha Aug. 8

Cornella Mar. 31
    Cornelia: Latin "practical; horn"

Corona: Spanish "crowned" May 14

Cotilla	Jan. 23
Credola	May 13
Crescentia: Spanish "crescent-faced; smiling"	June 15
Crescencia	
Crispina: Latin "curly-haired girl"	Dec. 5
Cunegundes	Mar. 3
Cunegunda	
Cuthberta	Mar. 20
Cynthia: Greek, English	Feb. 8
Cyra: American "willing"	Aug. 3
Cyrenia	Nov. 1
Cyrena: "siren"	
Cyria	June 5
Cyriaca	Mar. 20
Cyriana	Nov. 1
Cyrilla: Latin "royal", Greek "mistress, lady"	Oct. 28

D

Dafrosa	Jan. 4
Dagila	July 12
Daire: "outgoing"	Nov. 2
Daisy (Margaret): English "flower and day's eye"	June 10
Damaris: Latin, Greek "calm; calf; to tame; gentle" **Demara**	Oct. 4
Damiana: "one who soothes"	Apr. 12
Daniela: "judged by God alone" **Danette, Danila, Danita**: "gregarious"	July 21
Daphne: Greek "pretty nymph; laurel tree"	July 13
Daretia	July 19
Daria: Greek, Italian "rich woman of luxury" **Darice**: English "contemporary"	Oct. 25
Datiana	May 31
Dativa: Hebrew "believer"	Dec. 6
Dauphine	Nov. 26
Davida: Hebrew "beloved one" **Davina**: Hebrew "believer; beloved"	Dec. 29
Deborah: Hebrew "prophetess; bee"	Sept. 1
Deidre: Irish "sparkling" **Deirdre**: Irish, Gaelic "broken-hearted, sorrowful"	Jan. 15
Delia (Cordelia): Greek "lovely" **Della**: Greek "kind", German "noble"	Oct. 22
Delphine: Latin "swimmer", Greek "dolphin" **Delfina, Delphina**: Greek "dolphin; smart"	Dec. 9
Demetria: Greek	June 21

Denise (Dennis): French "wine-lover; follower of Dionysius"   Nov. 17
    Denice, Denys

Dephuta   Mar. 20

Desiree (Desiderius): French "desired"   May 23
    Desirata

Devota   Jan. 27

Diana: Latin "divine woman"   June 9
    Diane: Latin "divine"

Didara   June 23

Digna: Latin "worthy"   June 14

Dina (Geraldine): Hebrew, Scottish "right; royal"   Oct. 13

Dionysia: Latin "follower of Dionysius"   Dec. 12
    Dionetta, Dionisia, Diona: Greek "divine woman"

Doda   Apr. 24

Dolores (*Our Lady of Sorrows*): Spanish "sorrows"   Sept. 15
    Delores: Spanish, Latin "sorrows", **Dolora, Dolorita, Deloris**

Domaine   May 20

Dominica: Latin "follower of God"   July 6

Domna   Dec. 28

Domnina   Apr. 14

Donalda: Scottish "loves all", Scottish, Gaelic "world mighty"   July 15

Donata: Italian "celebrating", Latin "given"   Dec. 31
    Dona: Latin "always giving; lady", **Donna**: Italian "ladylike and genteel"

Donatilla   July 30

Donvina   Aug. 23

Dorcas: Greek "gazelle"   Oct. 25
    Dorcea: Greek "sea girl", **Dorcia**

Dorothy: Greek "gift of God"   Feb. 6

    Dora: Greek "gift", **Doralia, Doralice, Doralis, Doralise, Dore**: Irish "comptemplative", **Dorea, Dorelia, Dorena, Doretta**: Greek "gift from God", **Dorette, Doria**: Greek "secrets; gift", **Dorice, Dorinda**: Greek, Spanish, **Dorinna, Doris**: Greek "sea-loving; sea nymph; gift", **Dorissa, Dorita, Dorlisa, Dorna, Dorothea**: Greek "gift from God", **Dot**: Greek "spunky", **Dotty, Dolly**: American "effervescent"

Drusilla: Latin "strong"   Sept. 22

    Drucilla

Dula   Mar. 25

Dulcelina   Oct. 26

    Dulcea, Dulcia, Dulcie, Dulcina, Dulcyna

Dympna   May 15

E

Eanswide	Sept. 12
Eberta (Egbert)	Apr. 24
Edana: Irish "flaming energy"	July 5
Edberga	June 15
Eden (Aedan): Hebrew "paradise of delights; pleasure"	May 2
Edith: English "a blessed girl who is a gift to mankind; spoils of war" **Edita, Editha, Edyth**	Sept. 16
Edmunda: English "rich" **Edmee**: American "spontaneous", **Edmonda**	Nov. 20
Edna (Edana): Hebrew "youthful; pleasure"	July 5
Edwarda **Edwardina, Edwardine**	Oct. 13
Edwina: English "prospering female; rich in friendship"	Oct. 12
Egberta	Apr. 24
Egena	May 18
Eleanor: Greek "light-hearted; shining light" **Eleanora**: Greek "light", **Eleanore**: Greek, German "light and bright", **Eleonor**	Aug. 16
Electa: Greek "resilient and bright"	Oct. 21
Elena: Greek, Russian, Italian, Spanish "light and bright; beautiful"	Nov. 4
Elenara	May 2
Elene (Helen)	Aug. 18
Elevara	Mar. 28
Elevetha	Aug. 1
Elfrida: Greek "peaceful ruler", German "peaceful spirit" **Elfreda**	Dec. 8
Elia	Oct. 25

Elisabeth: Hebrew, French, German "sworn to God" July 8

Elizabeth: Hebrew "God's promise" Nov. 5
Elisa, Elisabet, Elisabetta, Elise: French, English "soft-mannered", **Elisia, Elissa**: Greek "God-loving; from the blessed isles", **Eliza**: Irish "sworn to God", **Elsa**: Hebrew, Scandinavian, German "patient; regal", **Elsabet, Elsbeth, Elspeth**: Scottish, **Elna, Elora**: American "fresh-faced"

Ella: Greek "beautiful and fanciful", German "other, foreign" Oct. 27
Elletta, Ellette

Ellen (Helen): English "open-minded" Aug. 18
Eileen: Irish "bright and spirited", **Elaine**: French "shining light; dependable girl", **Ellin, Ellyn**

Elma: Greek "God's protection", Turkish "sweet" Apr. 15

Eloine (Eloi) Dec. 1

Eloise (Louise): German "high-spirited" Jan. 31

Elvara Mar. 28

Elvira: Latin, German "light-haired and quiet; truly foreign" Jan. 25

Emelia May 23

Emeline Oct. 27

Emerentiana Jan. 23
Emerentia

Emerita Sept. 22

Emiliana Jan. 5

Emily: German "poised", English "competitor", Latin "industrious, striving" Sept. 19
Emelin, Emelina, Emeline, Emelyn, Emilie: French "charmer", **Emmelia, Emmeline**

Emma: German "whole, complete", Irish "strong" Apr. 11

Emmelia May 30

Encratis Apr. 16
Engratia

Enid: Welsh "lively; life"   Aug. 1

Ennatha   Nov. 13

Enora: "careful"   Apr. 12

Enrica (Henry): Spanish "rules her household"   July 15
    Enrika

Epicharis   Sept. 27

Epiphana   July 12

Epistemis   Nov. 5

Erasma   Sept. 3

Erena   May 5

Erica (Eric): Scandinavian "complete ruler; honorable; leading others"   May 18
    Erika: Scandinavian

Ermelinda: Spanish "fresh-faced"   Oct. 29
    Erma: Latin "wealthy", German "complete"

Ernestina: German "serious; determined; having a sincere spirit"   Nov. 7
    Erna: English "knowing; earnest", **Ernesta**, **Ernestine**: English
    "having a sincere spirit"

Erotheides   Oct. 27

Esperanza (Hope): Spanish "hopeful; hope"   Aug. 1
    Esperance

Esprite   Aug. 7

Estelle: French "glowing star"   May 21

Esther: Persian "myrtle leaf", English "shining star"   July 1
    Easter, **Esthera**, **Estra**, **Estrella**: Latin "shining star"

Etha   May 5

Ethel: German "noble", English "class"   Jan. 12
    Ethelina: "noble"

Ethelburga   July 7

Ethelburge   Oct. 11
    Edilburge

Etheldreda	June 23
Ethelviva	June 25
Etta (Henry): German, English "energetic"	July 15
Eudocia: Greek "fine" **Eudosia**	Mar. 1
Eudoxia	Nov. 2
Eugenia: Greek "well-born; regal and polished" **Eugenie**	Dec. 25
Eulalia: Greek, Italian "spoken sweetly" **Eulalie**: Greek "well-spoken"	Feb. 12
Eulampia	Oct. 10
Eunice: Greek "joyful; winning; she conquers"	Oct. 28
Eunomia	Aug. 12
Euphemia: Greek "respected" **Effie**: Greek "of high morals", German "good singer"	Mar. 20
Euphrasia	Mar. 13
Euphrosina	May 7
Euphrosyna	Jan. 1
Euprepia	Aug. 12
Euralia	Dec. 10
Eurosia	June 25
Eusebia	Oct. 29
Eustella **Eustelle**	May 21
Eustochium	Sept. 28
Eustolia	Nov. 9
Euthalia	Aug. 27
Eutropia	June 15

Evangelista   Sept. 16
    Evangeline: "bringing joy"

Eve: French, Hebrew "first woman"   Dec. 19
    Evelina: Russian "lively", **Eveline, Evelien, Evelyn:** Norman,
    English "optimistic"

Exuperantia   Apr. 26

Exuperia   July 26

F

Fabia: Latin "fabulous; special"   Jan. 20
   Fabiana, Fabienne: French "farming beans"

Fabiola: Latin, Spanish "royalty"   Dec. 27

Faila   Mar. 3

Faina   May 18

Faith: English "loyal woman; loyalty; belief"   Aug. 1
   Fay: Old French**, Faye:** English, French "light-spirited"**, Fayette:** Old French "little fairy"

Fanchea   Jan. 1

Fanchette (Frances)   Oct. 4
   Fanchon: French

Fara (Burgundofara)   Apr. 3

Farica: German "peaceful ruler; leader"   July 18

Fausta   Sept. 20

Faustina: Italian "lucky"   Jan. 18
   Faustine: Latin "fortunate, enjoying good luck"

Febronia   June 25

Fedora (Theodra): Greek "God's gift"   Apr. 1

Fedosia (Theodosia)   Apr. 2

Felicia: Latin "joyful; lucky, fortunate, happy"   Oct. 5
   Felice: Latin "happy"**, Felise:** German "joyful"**, Felita**

Felicissima   Aug. 12

Felicita: Spanish "gracious"   Mar. 6
   Felicity: Latin "happy girl"

Felicitas   Nov. 23

Felicula   Feb. 14

Felipa (Philippa)   Sept. 20
   Filipa, Felisa

Fenella: Irish, Gaelic "white; white shoulder"   Nov. 13

Ferdinanda   May 30
    Fernanda: Old German "adventurous; bold journey", **Fernande**

Fidelia: Italian "faithful"   Mar. 23

Fidelity (Fidelis): Latin "loyal"   Apr. 24

Fifi (Josephine): French "jazzy"   Oct. 23

Filomena (Philomena): Italian, Polish "beloved"   Aug. 11

Firmina   Nov. 24

Flavia: Latin "light-haired; yellow hair"   May 7

Flaviana   Oct. 5

Flora: Latin "flower", Spanish "flowering"   Nov. 24
    Florella: Latin "girl from Florence; blooming", **Floretta, Floria, Floris, Flossie**: English "grows beautifully"

Florence: Latin "flowering, in bloom", Italian "flourishing and giving"   Nov. 10
    Florencia, Florentia, Florinda

Florentina   June 20

Floreta   Aug. 22

Florida: Latin "flowered"   Aug. 29

Florina   May 1

Flotilda   Dec. 25

Fonilla   Jan. 17

Fortuna: Latin "good fortune"   Feb. 22
    Fortune: Latin "good fate"

Fortunata   Oct. 14

Foruntia   Apr. 27

Franca: Italian "free spirit"   Apr. 27

Frances: Latin "free; of French origin" Mar. 9

> **Fanchette, Fanchon**: French "from France", **Fanchonette, Fanny**: Latin "from France; bold", **France**: "French girl", **Francella, Francesca**: Italian "smiling", **Francine**: French "beautiful", **Francisca, Franny**: English "friendly"

Francha Apr. 25

Freda (Fredrick): German "serene; peaceful" July 18

> **Fredella**: "striking", **Frederica**: German "peaceful ruler; peacemaking", **Fredrika, Freida**: German "graceful", **Frida**: Scandinavian "lovely", **Fritzi**: German "leads in peace"

Frideswide Oct. 19

Fructuosa: Latin "bountiful; fruitful" Aug. 23

Fusca Feb. 13

G

Gabriella: Italian, Spanish "God is her strength"   Mar. 24
  Gabrielle: French, Hebrew "strong, by faith in God; heroine of God", **Gavrila, Gabriele, Gabriela**

Gadola   May 6

Gaiana   Sept. 30

Gaiola   Mar. 3

Galalia   Dec. 10

Galata   Apr. 19

Galena: Latin "metal; tough"   Feb. 10

Galla   Oct. 5

Galonia   July 24

Garda (Hildegarde)   Apr. 30

Gaudentia   Aug. 30

Gavina: Latin "from Gaibo"   May 6

Gemina   Jan. 4

Gemma: Latin, Italian, French "gem, jewel"   Apr. 11

Generosa: Spanish "generous"   July 17

Genesia   Aug. 25

Genevieve: German, French "high-minded"   Jan. 3
  Genever, Genevra, Guinevere: Welsh "queen; white; fair one; smooth, soft", **Ginevra:** Italian "fair one", **Geneva:** Old French "juniper tree", **Genovefa, Guenevere:** Welsh "soft; white"

Genoise   Dec. 23

Gentile   Jan. 28

Georgia: Greek, English "southern; cordial"   Feb. 15
  Georgetta, Georgette: French "lively and little", **Georgiana:** English "bright-eyed", **Georgina:** Greek, English "earthy", **Georgine**

Geralda	Mar. 13
Geraldina, Geraldine: French, German "spear ruler; strong", **Gerelda, Gerlinda, Giralda**	
Gerberta	Dec. 19
Germaine: French "of German origin; important"	June 15
Germana	Jan. 19
Gertrude: German "beloved; strong spear"	Nov. 16
Gertruda, Gerty	
Gilberta (Gilberte): German "smart"	Feb. 4
Gilda (Gildas): English "gold-encrusted; gilded"	Jan. 29
Gisele: French "devoted friend"	May 7
Giselle: Old German "pledge; hostage", **Gisella**	
Gladys: Welsh "flower; princess"	Mar. 29
Glaphyra	Jan. 13
Gloria: Latin "glorious; glory"	May 10
Gloriana, Glorianna, Glory: Latin "shining"	
Glyceria	May 13
Glitheria, Glycere	
Godeleva	July 6
Godelieva, Godelieve	
Godina	Feb. 15
Goldie (Aura): English "bright and golden girl"	July 19
Golinia	July 6
Gorgonia	Dec. 9
Grace: Latin "graceful; favor; blessing"	July 5
Gracia, Gratia: Scandinavian "graceful; gracious", **Gratiana**	
Gracilian	Aug. 12
Graecina	June 16
Grata	May 1

Gregoria: Latin "watchful; vigilant" — Nov. 17

Gresinda — July 25

Greta (Margaret): German "a pearl" — June 10
    Gretchen, Grethel, Grita, Gret, Gredel, Gretel: German "pearl; fanciful"

Guadalupe (*Our Lady of Guadalupe*): Spanish "easygoing; wolf valley" — Dec. 12

Gudelia — Sept. 29
    Gudela

Guenna: Welsh "soft" — Aug. 19

Guida (Guy): Italian "guide" — Sept. 12

Guilette (William) — June 25
    Guillena

Giuseppa (Josephine) — Oct. 23

Guiteria — May 22

Gundenes — July 18

Gwen: Welsh "happy; blessed" — July 5
    Gwenn

Gwendolene — Oct. 18
    Gwendolen, Gwendolin, Gwendoline, Gwendolyn: Welsh "fair bow; blessed ring; bright"

Gytha — Feb. 15

H

Haberilla **Habrilla**	Jan. 30
Halena: Russian "staunch supporter"	June 17
Hallie (Henry): German "high-spirited" **Hally**	July 15
Hannah (Anne): Hebrew "merciful; God-blessed; favored grace"	July 26
Harolda (Harold) **Harelda**: "rules the army"	Mar. 25
Harriet (Henry): French "homebody", German "estate or home ruler" **Hariett, Harrietta, Hattie, Hatty**: English "home-loving"	July 15
Hedda: German "capricious; warring"	July 7
Hedwig: Old German "contention, strife" **Hedy**: German "mercurial", Greek, Hebrew "delightful, sweet; my echo", **Hedwiges**	Oct. 17
Heira	Feb. 21
Helconides	May 28
Helen: Greek "beautiful and light; sun ray; shining light" **Helena**: Greek "beautiful; ingenious", **Helene**: French "pretty but contentious", **Helenka**	Aug. 18
Helga (Olga): Anglo-Saxon "pious", Old German, Old Norse "holy, sacred; successful"	July 11
Helia: Greek "sun" **Heliada**	June 20
Heliana	June 8
Heliena	Apr. 20
Helmina (William)	June 25
Heloise (Louise): German "hearty", French "renowned fighter"	Jan. 31
Helsa (Elizabeth): Scandinavian "God-loving", Danish "God's promise"	Nov. 5

Henchen (Joanna)   May 24

Henedina   May 14

Henrica (Henry)   July 15
    Hendrica, Henrika, Henrita, Henryka, Henrietta: English,
    German "home-ruler", **Henriette, Henrieta, Hetty**: English "rules"

Heraclia   June 1

Herena   Feb. 25
    Herene

Herenia   Mar. 8

Herina   May 5

Herlanda   Mar. 22

Hermana (Herman)   Apr. 7
    Hermandine, Hermine

Hermione: Greek "messenger; earthly; sensual"   Sept. 4
    Hermia: Greek "messenger", **Herminia**: Spanish

Hesperia   Aug. 10

Hester (Esther): Greek "star"   July 1

Hilaria: Latin, Polish "merrymaker"   Aug. 12

Hilda: German "practical; battle woman", Scandinavian "fighter"   Nov. 17

Hildeberta   Apr. 4

Hildeburg   June 3

Hildegard: German, Scandinavian "steadfast protector"   Sept. 17
    Hildegarda, Hildegarde: Old German "battle stronghold"

Hildemara   Oct. 25

Hiltrude   Sept. 27

Hirena   Feb. 25

Hirmina   Dec. 24

Honesta   Oct. 18

Honora: Latin "honorable"   Apr. 12
    Honore

Honorata: Polish "respected woman"   Jan. 11

Honoria: Spanish "of high integrity; a saint"   Apr. 12

Hope: Old English "expectation; belief"   Aug. 1

Horta (Dorothy)   Feb. 6

Hortense: Latin "caretaking the garden"   Jan. 11

Huberta (Hubert): German "brilliant mind"   Nov. 3

Huette (Hugh): German "intellectual; intellect, mind"   Apr. 29
    Huguetta, Hugette

Hulda: Scandinavian "sweetheart", German, Hebrew "loved one; mole"   Apr. 10

Humbelina   Feb. 12
    Humbeline

Humility   May 22

Hyacinth: Greek "flower"   Jan. 30
    Hyacintha, Hyacinthe

Hypatia: Greek "highest"   June 17

I

Ia — Aug. 4

Iacolyn (James) — July 25

Ida: German "kind", Greek, English "hardworking; industrious" — Sept. 4
    Idelle: Celtic "generous", Welsh "bountiful", **Idette**: "serious worker"

Idea — Jan. 15

Ignatia — Feb. 1
    Ignacia: Latin "passionate; burning, ardent"

Illuminata — Nov. 29

Ilsa (Helen): Scottish "glowing" — Aug. 18
    Ilse: German "loves God", **Ilona**: Hungarian "beauty"

Imelda: German, Italian "universal battle; contentious" — May 12

Immaculata (*The Immaculate Conception*): Spanish "spotless" — Dec. 8

Imogene (*Shrine of the Blessed Virgin, at Imogene, France*): Celtic, Latin "girl who resembles her mother" — Sept. 8
    Imogen: Irish, Gaelic "maiden"

Imperia: Latin "imperial; stately" — Sept. 6

Indica — May 9

Inez: Spanish "lovely" — Nov. 8
    Ines: Spanish "chaste"

Ingrid: Scandinavian "beautiful" — July 1
    Inga

Inista (Agnes) — Jan. 21

Innocensia: "innocent" — Feb. 1
    Innocentia

Iolana (Yolando): Hawaiian "violet; pretty; to soar like a hawk" — Dec. 28
    Iolanda

Ionilla — Jan. 17

Iphigenia: Greek "sacrifice"	Sept. 21
Iraidea	Sept. 5
Irais	Sept. 22
Irene: Greek "peace-loving" **Irena, Irina**: Greek, Russian "comforting"	Oct. 20
Irmina **Irma**: Latin "realistic", Old German "universal, complete"	Dec. 24
Isabel: Spanish "God-loving" **Isabeau, Isabella**: Spanish, Italian "dedicated to God", **Isabelle, Isbel, Isobel**	July 8
Isadora: Greek "beautiful; fertile" **Isidora**	Apr. 4
Ita: Irish "thirsts for knowledge; thirst"	Jan. 15
Ite	Jan. 15
Iva: Slavic "dedicated"	Oct. 27
Ivanna (John): Russian "gracious gift from God"	Dec. 27
Ivetta: "clever and athletic" **Iveta, Ivette**: French, **Ivy**: English, American "easygoing"	Jan. 13
Ivona (Yvonne): Slavic "gift"	May 19

J

Jacinta (Hyacinth): Spanish "hyacinth; sweet"   Jan. 30
    Jacintha, Jacinthe

Jacobina: Hebrew "he who supplants"   Aug. 1
    Jacobia

Jacqueline (James): French "little Jacquie; small replacement; he who   July 25
supplants"
    Jacobella, Jacquetta, Jaculin, Jamesina, Jamesine

Jane: Hebrew "the Lord is gracious"   Aug. 21
    Janel: French "dark eyes", **Janella**: "sporty", **Janet**: English "small;
forgiving", **Janette, Janetta, Janice**: Hebrew "knowing God's grace",
Johanna: German "the Lord is gracious", **Juanita**: Spanish "believer
in a gracious God; forgiving"

Janilla   Jan. 17

Januaria   Mar. 2

Jeanne: "God loving and gracious"   May 21

Jeonilla   Jan. 17

Jeremia: Hebrew "the Lord is exalted"   Jan. 21

Jessica (Joanna): Hebrew "rich; He sees"   May 24
    Jessie: Scottish "casual"

Jill (Julia): English "high-energy and youthful", Latin "youthful"   May 22

Joan: Hebrew "heroine; God-loving; the Lord is gracious"   May 30

Joanna: Hebrew "kind"   May 24
    Jean: Hebrew "the Lord is gracious", **Jeanette, Jenifer**: "fair-haired;
beautiful perfection", **Jeanie**

Jobina (Job): Hebrew "hurting"   May 10

Jocelyn: Latin "joyful"   Mar. 17
    Jocelin, Joceline, Josslyn

Jocunda   June 2

Jolenta   Mar. 6

Joletta (Viola): American "happy-go-lucky"   May 3
 Jolietta

Jonella   Jan. 16
 Jonila

Josepha   Feb. 14

Josephine: Hebrew "Jehovah increases", French "blessed" Oct. 23
 Josephina: "fertile"

Jovita: Latin "glad; made glad"   Feb. 15

Joy (Jucunda): Latin "joyful"   July 27

Joyce (Jucunda): Latin "joyous"   July 27

Juana   Dec. 8

Juanita: Spanish "believer in a gracious God; forgiving" Aug. 21

Jucunda   July 27

Judith: Hebrew "woman worthy of praise"   Sept. 14
 Juditha, Judithe, Judy

Julia: Latin "forever young"   May 22
 Julchen, Jule, Joli, Juliane, Julianna, Julianne, Juliet: Italian
 "loving", **Julietta, Julita**

Juliana: Italian, German, Spanish "youthful"   Feb. 7

Julie: English "young and vocal"   July 12

Juliette: French "romantic"   May 18

Julitta   June 16

June (Junia): Latin "born in June"   Nov. 14

Junella   Jan. 17

Junilla   Feb. 16

Justa   July 19

Justilla   Aug. 28

Justina: Latin "honest"   Apr. 14
 Justine: Italian, Latin "fair, upright"

K

Karen (Katherine): Greek, Irish "pure-hearted"   April 30
    Kara: Danish, Greek "beloved; dearest", **Karena, Kalina**: Hawaiian "unblemished", Slavic "flower", **Karin**: Scandinavian "kind-hearted", **Karina**: Russian "best of heart", Latin "even", **Kasia, Kassia, Katrina**: German "melodious", **Kathleen**: Irish "brilliant; unflawed", **Katheryn, Katarina**: Greek "pure", **Katinka, Katrien, Kitty**: Greek

Karla (Charles): German "bright-eyed", Greek "free man"   Nov. 4

Karoline: German   Nov. 4

Katherine (Catherine): Greek "powerful; pure"   Apr. 30
    Kathryn: English "powerful and pure", **Krina, Kathy**: English "pure", Irish "spunky"

Kayne   Oct. 8

Kennera   Oct. 29

Kenwyn   Oct. 8

Kerstin (Christina): Scandinavian "a Christian"   July 24
    Kirstie: Scandinavian "irrepressable", **Kisten, Kristina**: Greek "anointed"; Scandinavian "Christ's follower", Czechoslovakian

Keverne   Nov. 18

Keyna   Oct. 8

Kilda   Nov. 1

Kim (Korean martyrs): English, Vietnamese "precious metal; gold; sharp"

Kinga   July 24

L

Lamberta **Lambertina, Lambertine**	Sept. 17
Lancia	Aug. 18
Landine **Landoline**	Jan. 16
Languida	Oct. 21
Latina	June 2
Laura: Latin "the bay; laurel-crowned; joyous"	Oct. 19

    Laure, Laurena, Laurene, Laureen: American "old-fashioned", **Lauretta**: American "graceful", **Laurette**: American "graceful", **Laurine, Laurice, Lorita, Lora**: Latin "regal", **Loris**: Greek, Latin "fun-loving", **Laurinda**

Laurentia **Laurentina, Loraine**	Oct. 8
Laverne: Latin "breath of spring" **LaVerne, Lavernne**	Sept. 17
Lea: Hawaiian "goddess-like"	Mar. 22
Leda: Greek	Mar. 27
Lee (Elizabeth): English "meadow or pasture", Chinese "light-footed"	Nov. 5
Legissima	Apr. 27
Lelia: Arabic "beauty of the night"	Aug. 11
Lelica **Lela**: Kiswahili "black beauty", French "loyalty"	Feb. 12
Lena (Helen): Latin "siren" **Lenchen, Lenia**	Aug. 18
Lene	Nov. 12

Lenora (Helen)   Aug. 18
    Lenore: Greek "radiant", **Leon, Leora**: Greek "compassion; light-hearted", **Lonie**: American "beauty", **Leonora**: English, Greek "compassion; bright light", **Leonore**: Greek "glowing light"

Leocadia   Dec. 9

Leocritia   Mar. 15

Leona (Leo): Greek, Latin "lion; brave-hearted"   Apr. 11
    Leola: Latin "fierce; lionine", **Leonie**: Latin "lionlike; fierce"

Leonice   Mar. 1

Leonides   June 15

Leonilla   Jan. 17

Leonita   Mar. 1
    Leontina, Leontine

Leontia   Dec. 6

Leopolda   Apr. 2
    Leopoldina: "brave"

Letitia: Latin "joy"   Dec. 25
    Leticia: Latin, Spanish "joyful woman", **Letty, Lettie**: Latin, Spanish "happy"

Libaria   Oct. 8

Libera   Jan. 18

Liberata   Jan. 18

Liberty: Latin "free and open; freedom"   Feb. 3

Libya   June 15

Liceria   May 11

Lidia: Greek: "pleasant spirit"   Mar. 27

Lidwina: Scandinavian "the people's friend"   Apr. 14
    Lydwid

Liliosa   July 27

Lillian: Latin "pretty as a lily"   July 17
   Lila: Arabic "night; playful", **Lili, Lilah, Liley, Lilia**: American "flowing", **Lilis, Lilisa, Lillie, Lillien, Lillis, Lilly, Lily**: Latin, Chinese "elegant"

Lina: Greek, Latin, Arabic "palm tree", Scottish "light of spirit; lake calm"   Aug. 18

Linda (Ermelinda): Spanish "pretty girl"   Oct. 29

Lioba   Sept. 28

Lisa (Elizabeth): Hebrew, American "dedicated and spiritual"   Nov. 5
   Libby: Hebrew "bubbly", **Lise**: German "solemn", **Lisetta, Lisette**: French "little Elizabeth", **Lisi, Lisbeth**: Hebrew

Lolita (Dolores): Spanish "sorrows"   Sept. 15
   Loleta

Lollia   June 23
   Lollie

Lorena: English "photogenic"   Aug. 10
   Lorna: Latin "laurel-crowned; natural"

Lorenza: Laitn "wears laurel wreath", Italian "from Laurentum"   Oct. 8

Loretta (*Shrine of Our Lady of Loretta—Italy*): English "large-eyed beauty" Dec. 10

Lottie (Charlotte): American "old-fashioned"   Nov. 4
   Lotta: Swedish "sweet"

Louisa: English "patient"   Jan. 31
   Luisa: Spanish "smiling", **Luise**

Louise: German "hardworking and brave; renowned fighter"   Mar. 15
   Lois: Greek "good; superior", **Lou, Louison, Lulu**: Swahili, Tanzanian, Hawaiian "precious; pearl; calm", German, English "kind", **Lola**: Spanish "pensive"

Lourdes (*Our Lady of Lourdes—France*): French "hallowed"   Feb. 11

Lucasta: Spanish "bringer of light"   June 27

Lucella   May 10

Luchina   Aug. 23

Lucia: Italian, Greek, Spanish "light; lucky in love"   Mar. 26

Luciana: Italian "fortunate" — May 18

Lucida — Jan. 3

Lucilla: English "bright" — July 29

Lucina: American "happy" — June 30

Lucosa — Sept. 28

Lucretia: Latin "wealthy woman; succeed" — Nov. 23
    Lucrece

Lucy: Latin, Scottish, Spanish "light-hearted; light" — Dec. 13
    Luce, Lucie: French, American "lucky girl", **Lucetta:** English "radiating joy", **Lucille:** English "bright-eyed", **Lucinda:** Latin "prissy", **Lucya**

Ludmilla: Slavic "beloved one; graceful people" — Sept. 16

Ludovica — Jan. 31

Luella (Louise-Ella): German "conniving" — Aug. 25
    Louella: English "elf"

Lunette — Aug. 1

Lupe (Guadalupe): Spanish "enthusiastic" — Dec. 12

Lutgard — June 16

Lydia: Greek "musical; unusual; from Lydia" — Aug. 3

M

Mabilia	Nov. 21
Mabele, Mabelle, Maybelle, Mabel: Latin "well-loved", English "lovable"	
Macaria: Spanish, Greek "blessed"	Apr. 8
Macaire	
Macra	Jan. 6
Macrina	Jan. 14
Madeleine: French "high-minded"	May 25
Madonna (*In honor of Our Blessed Mother*): Latin "my lady; spirited"	Oct. 11
Magda (Margaret): Scandinavian "believer"	June 10
Magdalen	July 22
Madalene, Madalena, Madeline: Hebrew "woman from Magdala", **Madalyn, Madel, Madelon, Magdala:** Greek "girl in the tower", **Magdalene:** Greek, Scandinavian "spiritual", **Magdelaine, Marlina, Marlene:** Greek "high-minded; attractive", English "adorned"	
Magina: Russian "hard-working"	Dec. 3
Magita	Sept. 8
Magna	May 6
Majella (Gerard Majella)	Oct. 16
Malina: Scandinavian "in the tower", Hawaiian "peace"	Apr. 28
Mamelta	Oct. 17
Mandie (Amanda)	June 18
Manda: American "beloved"	
Mannea	Aug. 27
Manon (Mary): French "exciting"	Dec. 8
Manette	
Manuelita (Manuel)	June 17
Manuela: Spanish "sophisticated girl"	

Marana	Aug. 3
Marca (Mark)	Apr. 25
Marcella: Latin "combative"	Jan. 31
Marcel, Marcele, Marcelle, Marcellina	
Marchell	Sept. 5
Marcia: Latin, American "combative"	Mar. 3
Marciana	Jan. 9
Marcina	June 8
Marcionilla	Jan. 9
Mardia	Oct. 22
Marella	May 21
Mareme	Nov. 22
Marga	Apr. 6
Margaret: Greek, Scottish, English "treasured pearl; pure-spirited"	June 10

    Madge, Magde, Marfa, Margareta, Margetta: Spanish "pearl", **Margarita**: Italian, Spanish "winning", **Margarta, Margery, Margo, Margory, Marjorie**: Greek, English, Scottish "bittersweet; pert", **Marjory, Margala, Margola, Marsali, Maggie**: Greek, English, Irish "priceless pearl", **Maisie**: Scottish "treasure"

Marianna	Apr. 17
Mariana: Spanish "quiet girl", **Marianne**	
Marina: Latin "sea-loving; from the sea"	June 18
Marita	Mar. 16
Marsilia	Apr. 8
Martana	Dec. 2
Martha: Aramaic "lady; mistress of the house"	July 29
Marta: Danish "treasure", **Martel, Martella, Marthine**	
Martia	June 21
Martina: Latin, German "combative"	Jan. 30
Martine: French "combative"	

Mary: Latin "star of the sea" Sept. 12

    Mara: Hebrew "bitter", Greek "thoughtful believer", **Marea, Mare**: American "living by the ocean", **Marella, Mair**: Irish "religious", **Maire, Marise**: Japanese "infinite, endless", **Mariel**: German "spiritual", **Marla**: English, German "believer; easygoing", **Maret**: English "bittersweet", **Marei, Mae**: English "bright flower", **May**: Old English "bright flower; the fifth month", **Maraline, Maria**: Latin, French, German, Italian, Polish, Spanish "desired child", **Marie**: French "dignified and spiritual; star of the sea", **Marian**: English "thoughtful", **Mariane, Marien, Mari**: Welsh, Japanese "ball; round", **Mariella**: Italian "blessed", **Marintha, Marion**: French "delicate spirit", **Marionette, Marja, Marsia, Marya**: Arabic "white and bright", **Marusche, Mascha, Maureen, Maribel**: French, English, American, **Marilla**: "shining sea", **Marilyn**: Hebrew "fond-spirited", **Mayme, Mollie, Molly**: Irish "jovial"

Matilda: German "powerful fighter; mighty in battle" Mar. 14
    Machtilde, Mathilde, Matilde, Mathildis

Matrona Mar. 20

Matutina Mar. 27

Maude: English "old-fashioned" July 22
    Maud, Maudlin

Maura: Latin, Irish "dark" Nov. 30
    Maure

Mauritia Sept. 22

Maxentia Nov. 20

Maxima Apr. 8

Maximilla Feb. 19

Maxine (Maximillian): Latin "greatest of all" Oct. 12

Mayra: Spanish "flourishing; creative" July 28

Mazota Dec. 23

Melania: Italian "giving; philanthropic" Dec. 31
    Melanie: Greek "dark; sweet; black; dark-skinned", **Melani, Melany**

Melinda (Ermelinda): Latin "honey; sweetheart" Oct. 29

Melita (*Our Lady of Mount Carmel*): Greek "honey-sweet"   July 16

Melitina   Sept. 15

Menodora   Sept. 10

Mercedes (*Our Lady of Mercy*): Spanish "merciful; rewarded"   Sept. 24
    Merced, Mercy: English "forgiving; compassion", **Merry**: English "joyful, lighthearted; cheerful"

Mercuria   Dec. 12

Merita   Sept. 22

Messina: Arabic "middle"   Apr. 19

Metrodora   Sept. 10

Michele (Michael): Italian, French, American "God-loving"   Sept. 29
    Michelle: French, Hebrew "who resembles God", **Michon, Miguela**: Hebrew "who resembles God", **Michaela**: Hebrew "God-loving"

Milburga   Feb. 23

Mildred: English "gentle; gentle strength"   July 13
    Millie: English, **Milly**

Milissa: Greek "softspoken"   Mar. 16
    Milice

Mimi (Wilhelmina): French "willful"   Mar. 24
    Minna: German "sturdy"

Mina (Wilhelmina): German, Polish "resolute protector; willful"   June 25
    Minette: French "loyal woman"

Minerva: Latin "the mind", Greek "bright; strong"   Oct. 25

Miriam (Mary): Hebrew "living with sadness"   Sept. 12

Mitrina   Aug. 8

Modesta   Nov. 4
    Modesty: Latin "modest, without conceit"

Modwenna   July 5

Moira (Myron): English, Irish "pure; great one"   Aug. 8

Monegundes   July 2

Monessa	Sept. 4
Monica: Greek "seeking company of others"	May 4
Mona: Greek "shining-cheeked", Irish, Gaelic "noble, aristocratic", **Monique**: French "saucy; advisor"	
Monice	Apr. 16
Monna	Nov. 26
Montana: Latin "mountain"	May 25
Murenna	May 26
Muriel (Myron): Celtic "shining", Irish, Gaelic "sparkling, shining sea"	Aug. 8
Mergl, Meriel: Irish "girl who shines like the sea", **Myra**: Greek "myrrh", Latin "fragrant", **Mira**: Latin, Slavic, Hindi "wonderful; peace; prosperous", Spanish "wonderful girl", **Mirilla, Myrilla**	
Murina	May 27
Mustiola	July 3
Myrope	July 13
Myrtle (Murial): Greek "loving"	Aug. 8

N

Nabara	Oct. 18

Nadine (Hope): Russian, French "dancer" Aug. 1
    Nada: Arabic "morning dew; giving"

Nancy (Anne): English, Irish "generous woman" July 26
    Nanette: French "giving and gracious", **Nanon**: French "slow to anger", **Nanna**: Scandinavian "brave", **Nanelia**

Narcissa: Greek "daffodil" Mar. 18

Natalia: Russian, Latin "born on Christmas; beauty" Dec. 1

Natalie: Latin "born on Christmas" July 27
    Natasha: Latin, Russian "glorious; born on Christmas", **Natica**

Nathania (Nathaniel): Hebrew "God has given" Aug. 24

Nell (Cornelia): English "sweet charmer" Mar. 31
    Neala: Irish "spirited", Gaelic "champion", **Nelia**: Hebrew "closing, locking", Spanish "yellow-haired", **Nella, Nelle, Nellis, Nelly, Nellie, Nelena**

Neomisia Sept. 25

Nessa: Irish "devout" July 10
    Nessia

Neysa (Agnes) Jan. 21

Nice Apr. 16

Nicea Aug. 29

Niceras Dec. 27

Niceta July 24

Nicolette (Nicholas): French "a tiny Nicole; little beauty" Dec. 6
    Nichola, Nicolina

Nimmia Aug. 12

Nina (Anne): Russian, Hebrew "little girl; great-granddaughter", Spanish July 26
"bold girl"
    Ninetta: American "cloud", **Ninon**: French "feminine"

Nirilla	May 21
Nita (Joan): Hebrew	May 30
Noel (*Nativity of Our Lord*): Latin "born on Christmas"	Dec. 25
Noella, Nielle	
Nominanda	Dec. 31
Nona: Latin "ninth; knowing"	Oct. 31
Nonna	Aug. 5
Nora (Eleanor): Greek, Scandinavian, Scottish "light; bright; from the north"	Aug. 16
Norah (Honora)	Apr. 12
Noreen: Irish, Latin "acknowledging others", **Norena, Norine**	
Norma: Latin "gold standard"	Aug. 5
Norrice	Aug. 25
Novella: Latin "new"	Apr. 12
Nunciata	Mar. 25
Nunilo	Oct. 22
Nympha	Nov. 10
Nymphodora	Mar. 13

O

Obdulia	Sept. 5
Octavia: Latin "eighth child; born on eight day of the month; musical"	Apr. 15
Odella: Hebrew, Greek "singer of spiritual songs"	Feb. 12
Odilia: Spanish "wealthy" **Odile**: French "sensuous"	Dec. 4
Ola (Olaf): Old Norse, Hawaiian, Nigerian "ancestor's relic; life, well-being; precious", Scandinavian "bold"	July 29
Olga: Old Norse, Scandinavian, Russian "blessed, holy woman; successful"	July 11
Olive: Latin "subtle" **Oliva**	June 3
Olivia: English "flourishing", Latin "olive tree"	June 10
Olympias **Olympia**: Greek "heavenly woman; from Mount Olympus"	Dec. 17
Onesta (Honesta)	Oct. 18
Onora (Honora): Latin "honorable; honor"	Apr. 12
Oona (Winifred): Latin "one alone"	Nov. 3
Oranda	Sept. 15
Orlanda (Orlando): German "celebrity"	May 20
Osith	Oct. 7
Otilie: Czech "fortunate girl" **Othilia, Ottilia**	Dec. 13

P

Pacifica: Spanish "peaceful"	Mar. 24
Palagia	Oct. 8
Palladia	May 24
Pamela (Helen): Greek "sweet as honey"	Aug. 18
Pandonia	Aug. 26
Parasceves	Mar. 20
Paris: French "graceful woman"	Aug. 5
Patience: English "woman of patience; enduring, forebearing"	May 1
Patricia: Latin "woman of nobility; unbending" **Patrice**: French "svelte"	Aug. 25
Paula: Latin "small and feminine" **Pala**: Native American "water", **Poila, Paule, Pauline**: Latin "precocious", **Paulette**: French "little Paula", **Paulita**	Jan. 26
Paulina: Latin "small", Italian "lovely"	Dec. 31
Pearl (Margaret): Latin "jewel from the sea" **Peggy**: Greek "pearl; priceless"	June 10
Pelagia: Polish "sea girl", Greek "of the sea"	June 9
Penelope (Irene): Greek "patient; weaver of dreams"	Oct. 20
Perpetua: Latin "forever, perpetual", Spanish "lasting"	Mar. 6
Perseveranda	June 26
Persia: "colorful"	Feb. 8
Petrine (Peter): Scandinavian "rock" **Petrina**	June 29
Petronilla: Greek "rock; dependable" **Perette, Pernell**	May 31
Phara	Dec. 7
Philea	Nov. 17

Philene (Philo): Greek "loving others"   Apr. 25

Philippa: Greek "horse lover"   Sept. 20
    Philippina, Pippa: English "ebullient; horse-lover"

Philomena: Greek "beloved; powerful love", German "friend of strength" Aug. 11

Philonilla   Oct. 11

Phoebe: Greek "bringing light; bright, radiant"   Sept. 3
    Phebe

Photides   Mar. 20

Photina: "fashionable"   Mar. 20

Pia: Latin "devout, pious, reverent"   Jan. 19

Pientia   Oct. 11

Pierrette (Peter): Greek "reliable"   June 29

Placidia: Latin "calm, placid"   Oct. 11
    Placida: Latin "serenity"

Plautilla   May 20

Polly (Molly-Margaret): Irish "devout; joyous"   June 10

Polonia (Appolonia)   Feb. 9

Polyxena: "very hospitable"   Sept. 23

Pomposa   Sept. 19

Pontiana   Feb. 27

Potamias   Dec. 5
    Potamia

Potamioena   June 28

Praepedigna   Feb. 18

Praxedes   July 21

Prima: Latin "first; fresh"   Feb. 9

Primeva   Feb. 11

Primitiva   Feb. 24

Principia   May 11

Prisca: Latin "old spirit"   Jan. 18

Priscilla: Latin "wisdom of the ages; ancient, venerable"   Jan. 16
    Pricilla

Probata   May 10

Prosperia   June 25
    Prospera: Latin "does well"

Prudence: Latin "wise; careful; caution, discretion"   May 19
    Prudentia, Prue

Publia   Oct. 9

Pudentiana   May 19

Pulcheria: Italian "chubby; curvy"   Sept. 10

Pura (*Feast of the Purification*)   Feb. 2

Q

Quartilla	Mar. 19
Quieta	Nov. 28
Quinctilla	Mar. 19
Quinta: Latin "fifth day of the month"	Feb. 8
Quintina: Latin "fifth child"	
Quintilla: Latin "fifth girl"	Mar. 19
Quirilla	May 15
Quiteria	May 22

R

Rachel: Hebrew "peaceful as a lamb; ewe"   Sept. 2
   Rachela, Rachele, Rachelle: French "calm"

Radegund   Aug. 13

Radiana   Aug. 13

Ragnild: Teutonic "all-knowing power"   July 28

Rainalda   July 16
   Raineld

Raingarda   June 26

Raissa   Sept. 5

Ramona (Raymond): Teutonic "beautiful protector", Spanish, Old   Jan. 23
   German "protecting hands"

Raphaela: Hebrew "God heals; helping to heal"   Oct. 24
   Rafaela: Hebrew "spiritual"

Ravenna: English "blackbird"   July 23

Raymonda   Jan. 23

Rebecca: Hebrew "loyal; to bind"
   Reba: Hebrew "fourth-born"

Redempta   July 23

Regina: English, Latin "thoughtful; queen"   Sept. 7
   Regia, Reine: Spanish "queen", **Reinette, Reina**

Renata: Latin "reborn"   Mar. 16
   Renee: French "born again", **Rena**: Hebrew "joyful singer; melody"

Renelda   Mar. 22

Renie (Irene): Latin "renewal"   Oct. 20

Reparata   Oct. 8

Restituta   May 17

Revocata   Feb. 6

Reyne	Sept. 7
Richarda	Apr. 3
Richelia	Feb. 1
Richella	
Ripsimis	Sept. 29
Rita: Greek "precious pearl", Hindi "right"	May 22
Reta: African "shakes up"	
Ritza	Aug. 30
Roberta: English "brilliant mind", Old German "bright fame"	May 13
Robina: Scottish "birdlike; robin"**, Robenetta, Robenette, Robinia**	
Roderica: German "princess; famous ruler"	Mar. 13
Rogata	May 31
Rolanda: German "rich woman", Latin "renowned in the land"	Sept. 15
Rolenda	May 13
Rollande, Rollende	
Roma: Italian "girl from Rome; adventurous"	Jan. 21
Romana	Feb. 23
Romaine: French "daredevil; citizen of Rome"**, Romayne**	
Romula	July 23
Ronalda	Aug. 20
Rosalia: Italian "hanging roses"	July 15
Rosamond: English "beauty", Old German "horse protector"	Apr. 3
Rosanne (Rose-Anne)	July 26
Rosceline	June 11
Rosseline	

Rose: Latin "rose; blushing beauty"   Aug. 30
    Rosabel: "beautiful rose", **Rosabelle:** French "beautiful rose", **Rosalba:** Latin "glorious as a rose; white rose", **Rosalie:** English "striking dark beauty", French, **Rosalind:** Spanish "lovely rose", Old German "gentle horse", **Rosalinde, Rosaleen, Roseta, Rosetta:** Italian "longlasting beauty", **Rosette:** Latin "flowering; rosy", **Rosina:** English "rose", **Rosita:** Spanish "pretty", **Rosalyn, Rosamund, Roanna:** Spanish "brown skin", **Rosel, Roselle:** Latin "rose", **Rosemare, Rosina:** English "rose", **Rosamary**

Roseline   Jan. 17

Rosena   Mar. 17

Roseria (*Our Lady of The Rosary*)   Oct. 7

Rosula   Sept. 14

Roxanna: Persian "bright"   May 22
    Roxanne: Persian "lovely as the sun; dawn", **Roxane**

Ruby (Robert): French "precious jewel", English "the red gemstone"   May 13
    Rubetta

Rudolpha (Rudolph)   July 27
    Rudolfa

Rufina: Latin "red-haired"   July 10

Rustica   Dec. 31

Ruth: Hebrew "loyal friend; companion"   Sept. 1

S

Sabela: "spiritual"   Dec. 18

Sabina: Latin "desirable"   Aug. 29
    Sabine: Latin

Sacha (Alexander): Greek "helpful girl"   Feb. 26

Salaberga   Sept. 22

Sallustia   Sept. 14

Salome: Hebrew "peace"   June 29

Salomea   Nov. 17

Samina   June 2

Samuela: Hebrew "selected; God heard"   Aug. 20

Sancha: Spanish "sacred child"   Mar. 13

Sancta   Aug. 16

Sandra (Alexander): Greek "helpful; protective"   May 18

Santina   May 2

Sara: Hebrew "God's princess"   Dec. 10

Sarah: Hebrew "princess"   Dec. 23
    Sadie: Hebrew "charmer; princess", **Sally:** Hebrew "princess", **Sallie**,
    Sarita: Spanish "regal"

Sarapia   Aug. 29

Sarmatia   June 2

Sarona   May 28

Satira   May 10

Saturnina   June 4

Saula   Oct. 20

Savina: Latin   Jan. 30

Scholastica: Latin "rhetorician, orator"   Feb. 10

Sebastia	July 4
Sebastiana	Sept. 16
Secunda: Latin "second"	July 10
Secundilla	Mar. 2
Secundina	Jan. 15
Sedopha	July 5
Selina (Celestina): Greek "moon"	Sept. 22
Selena: Greek "like the moon; shapely", **Selene**: Greek	
Selma (Anselm): German "fair-minded female", Arabic "helmet of God; safe"	Apr. 21
Senorina	Apr. 22
Sentiana	May 20
Seraphina	July 29
Seraphine, Serafine, Serafina: Hebrew "ardent; burning ones"	
Serapia	July 29
Serena: Latin "calm; serene"	Aug. 16
Serotina	Dec. 31
Severa	July 20
Sharon (*Rose of Sharon*): Hebrew "open heart; desert plain; fertile plain"	
Sheila (Cecilia): Irish "woman; gorgeous", Gaelic "blind"	Nov. 22
Sheelar, Sheela: Hindi "gentle spirit"	
Sibylla (Sibyllina)	Mar. 23
Sibelle, Sibille, Sibil, Sibley: Anglo-Saxon "related", **Sibyl**: Greek "intuitive; prophetess, oracle", **Sibylle, Sibylla, Sybilla, Sybila, Sevilla**: Spanish	
Sidonia: French "spiritual", Latin "from Sidon"	Aug. 21
Sidonie: French "appealing"	
Silissa	Oct. 25
Silva	Dec. 15

Simona: Hebrew "svelte"   Feb. 18
    Simonette, Simone: French "wise and thoughtful", Hebrew "hear, listen"

Sirina   Aug. 26

Sopatra   Nov. 9

Sophia: Greek "wise one"   Sept. 30
    Sofia: Latin, **Sonia:** Slavic "effervescent", **Sonya:** Greek "wise", **Sophie:** Greek "intelligent"

Speranza (Hope): African "hope"   Aug. 1

Stasia (Anastasia): Greek, Russian "resurrection"   Dec. 25
    Stacie

Stanislawa   Aug. 15

Stella: Latin "bright star"   July 10

Stephanie: Greek "regal; crown, garland"   Dec. 26
    Stefana, Stefanie: Greek "regal"

Successa   Mar. 27

Sunniva   July 8
    Sunnifa

Susanna: Hebrew "gentle"   May 24
    Susan: Hebrew "lily; pretty flower", **Susanne, Susannah, Susie, Suzanna, Suzanne:** English "fragrant", **Susy, Suzette, Sue**

Sylvia: Latin "sylvan; girl of the forest; woods, forest"   Nov. 3
    Silvania, Silvia: Latin "deep; woods-loving", **Silvie, Sylwyn**

Symphorosa   July 2

Symphrosia   July 18

Syncletica   Jan. 5

Syria   June 8

T

Talida	Jan. 5
Tallulah: Native American "leaping water; sparkling girl"	June 6
Tallula	
Tama: Hebrew, Japanese "globe, ball; perfect"	Oct. 11
Tamasine (Thomas): English "twin"	Dec. 21
Tarasia	Sept. 3
Tarbula	Apr. 22
Tarsilla	Dec. 24
Tarsitia	Jan. 15
Tatiana: Russian "snow queen"	Jan. 12
Tatta	Sept. 25
Terentiana	July 10
Terentia	
Teresa: Greek "gardener; late summer"	Oct. 15

    Teresina, Terese: Greek "nurturing", **Terisia, Tess**: Greek "harvesting life", **Tessie, Theresa**: Greek "reaping a harvest", **Therese**: Greek "bountiful harvest", **Theresia, Tressa**: Greek "reaping life's harvest"

Tertulla	Apr. 29
Thadine (Thaddeus): "worthy of praise"	Oct. 28
Thais	Oct. 8
Tharsilla	Dec. 24
Thea	Dec. 19
Thecla	Sept. 23

    Tecla: Greek "God's glory", **Tekla**: Greek "legend; diving glory", **Thecle, Thekla**: Greek "famous"

Thecusa	May 18
Theda (Theodora): Old German "people; confident"	Apr. 1

Thelma (Anthelmius): Greek "giver; will, volition"　　　　June 26

Theoctistis　　　　Nov. 10

Theodora: Greek "sweetheart; God's gift"　　　　Apr. 28

Theodosia: Greek "God's gift"　　　　Apr. 2

Theodota　　　　July 17

Theonilla　　　　Aug. 23

Theophila: Greek "loved by God"　　　　Dec. 28

Theopistes　　　　Sept. 20

Thessalonica　　　　Nov. 7

Thomasina: Hebrew, Aramaic "twin"　　　　Dec. 21
　　　Tomasa, Thomasia, Thomasine

Thrasilla　　　　Dec. 24

Tilda (Matilda): German "powerful"　　　　Mar. 14
　　　Tillie: "cute; strong"

Timothea: Greek "honoring God; God's honor"　　　　Jan. 24

Tina (nickname for several names, eg. Christina, Martina, etc.): Latin, Spanish "little and lively"

Titiana　　　　July 17

Toscana　　　　Dec. 18
　　　Tosca: Italian "from Tuscany", **Toscaine**

Trina (Catherine): Greek "perfect; scintillating"　　　　Apr. 30
　　　Trine, Trinette

Triphina　　　　July 5

Trixie (Beatrice): English, Latin "personable"　　　　July 29
　　　Tryce

Trophe (Eutropia)　　　　Dec. 14

Trude (Gertrude)　　　　Nov. 16
　　　Trudel, Trudy: German "hopeful"

Tryphenna	Nov. 10
Tryphonia	Oct. 18
Tryphosa	Nov. 10

U

Udelina	Oct. 19
Uganda	June 3
Ulrica (Ulric): Old German "power of the wolf; power of the home; leader" **Ulrika**: Teutonic "leader", Scandinavian "wealthy ruler", **Ulrique**	July 4
Una (Winifred): Latin "unique; one"	Nov. 3
Urania: Greek "universal beauty; heavenly"	May 28
Urbana: Latin "born in the city; of the city"	May 17
Ursa: Greek, Latin "star; bear-like"	Oct. 26
Ursula: Latin, Scandinavian "little female bear" **Ursel, Ursele**	Oct. 21

V

Valdrada	May 5
Valentia	June 2
Valentine	
Valentina: Latin "romantic; strong, healthy"	July 25
Valeria: Spanish "having valor"	June 5
Valerie: Latin "robust"	
Valeriana	Nov. 15
Vanessa (Esther): Greek "flighty"	July 1
Vanora: Old Welsh "white wave; mercurial"	Jan. 3
Vaudree	May 5
Vaune	Nov. 9
Vendreda (Winifred)	June 5
Veneranda: "honored; venerable"	Nov. 14
Venetia (Beatrice): Latin "girl from Venice"	July 29
Venice: "coming of age"	
Venisa	July 12
Vera: Russian "faithful friend", Slavic, Latin "faith; truth"	Jan. 24
Verbetta	Sept. 16
Verdiana	Feb. 1
Veridiana	
Verena: English "honest", Latin "true"	Sept. 1
Verona: "flourishes; honest"	Aug. 29
Veronica: Latin "true image; real"	Jan. 13
Verenice, Veron, Venise	
Vestina	July 17
Vesta: Latin "home-loving"	
Vevette (Genevieve)	Jan. 3

Vicentia (Vincent)   Apr. 5

Victoria: Latin "winner"   Nov. 17

Victorina   Oct. 18
    Victorine

Victory: Latin "a winning woman"   Dec. 23
    Victoire, Victorie

Vidette (David): Hebrew "loved"   Dec. 29
    Vida: Hebrew, Spanish "life"

Vigilia: Latin "vigilant"   June 26

Vincentia: Latin "winner; prevailing"   Apr. 5

Viola: Latin "violet; lovely lady"   May 3
    Violante: Greek, Latin "purple flower", **Violet**: English, French "purple flower", Latin "purple", **Violetta, Violette**

Virginia (*In honor of The Blessed Virgin*): Latin "pure female; maiden"

Vissia   Apr. 12

Vitalina   Feb. 21

Viventia   Mar. 17

Vivian: Latin "bubbling with life"   Dec. 2
    Viva: Latin "alive; lively", **Vivien**: "bubbling with life", **Vivienne**

Vladislawa (Ladislaus)   June 27

W

Walburga: German "strong protection"   Feb. 25

Waltrude   Apr. 9

Wanda (Wando): Polish "wild; wandering", Slavic "the tribe of Vandals"   Apr. 17

Wenefride   Nov. 3
    Winefride

Wereburge   Feb. 3

Wilfreda: English "goal-oriented; desiring peace"   Sept. 9
    Wilfrida

Wilgefortis   July 20

Wilhelmina (William): German "able protector; determined protector"   June 25
    Willa: English "desirable", Old German "will helmet, protection",
    Wileen, Willabel, Willabelle, Wilhelmine, Wilette: "open",
    Williamina

Winifred: German "peaceful woman", Welsh, Old English "holy,   Nov. 3
    blessed reconciliation; joy and peace"
    Winfreda

Wivina   Dec. 17

X

Xantippa	Sept. 23
Xantippe: Greek	
Xaverie (Xavier)	Dec. 3
Xene	Jan. 24
Xenia: Greek "quest, stranger"	Sept. 23
Ximena (Simon): Spanish "peaceful"	Oct. 28
Xina (Christina)	July 24

Y

Yoland	Apr. 23
Yolaine	
Yolanda: Greek, Spanish "violet flower"	Dec. 28
Yolande, Yolanthe, Yolette	
Ysabeau (Isabel)	July 8
Ysabel: French, Spanish "clever"	
Ytha (Ita)	Jan. 15
Yvonne (Ivo): French "athletic", Old German "yew wood"	May 19
Yvette: French "lively archer"	

Z

Zandra (Alexander): Spanish, Greek "shy; helpful"   May 18

Zanetta (Joanna)   May 24

Zara (Sarah): Hebrew "dawn; glorious", Arabic "radiance"   Dec. 23

Zebina   Nov. 13

Zelina (Soline)   Oct. 17

Zenaides   June 5

Zenia (Xenia): Greek "open"   Sept. 23

Zenobia: Latin, Greek   Oct. 30

Zita: Spanish "rose", Arabic "mistress", Greek "seeker"   Apr. 27

Zoe: Greek "lively; vibrant; life"   July 5

Zona: Latin "funny; brash; girdle"   Feb. 9
   Zoa: Greek "life; vibrant"

Zosima   July 15

Bibliography

Butler, Rev. Alban. *The Lives of the Fathers, Martyres and Other Principal Saints: Volume I-IV.* London, Dublin and Belfast: Virtue & Co. LD., 1756; Great Falls, MT: St. Bonaventure Publications, 1997.

Campbell, Mike. "Behind the Name: The Etymology and History of First Names." *www.behindthename.com*

Connell, Rev. Francis J., C.SS.R., S.T.D., *The New Confraternity Edition Revised Baltimore Catechism and Mass No. 3.* Benziger Brothers, Inc., 1949. Colorado Springs, CO: The Seraphim Company, Inc., 1987.

Dunne, Rev. William P. *Is It a Saint's Name?* Rockford, IL: TAN Books and Publishers, Inc., 1977.

Jone, Fr. Heribert. *Moral Theology.* Westminster, MY: The Newman Press, 1962. Rockford, IL: TAN Books and Publishers, Inc., 1993.

Kelly, Rev. George A. *The Catholic Marriage Manual.* New York, NY: Random House, 1958.

McHugh, John A., O.P., S.T.M., Litt.D. and Charles J. Callan, O.P., S.T.M., Litt.D. *Catechism of the Council of Trent for Parish Priests.* South Bend, IN: Marian Publications, 1976. Rockford, IL: TAN Books and Publishers, Inc., 1982.

Morrow, Most Rev. Louis LaRavoire, D.D., *A Catechism in Pictures: My Catholic Faith, A Manual of Religion.* Louis LaRavoire Morrow International Copyright, 1949. Kansas City, MO: Sarto House, 2000.

"The Roman Martyrology." *www.breviary.net/martyrology/mart.htm*

Stafford, Diane. *50,001+ Best Baby Names*. Naperville, IL: Sourcebooks, Inc., 2004. (one of multiple sources for name meanings)

"Think Baby Names." *www.thinkbabynames.com*

Weiser, Fr. Francis X., S.J. *Religious Customs in the Family: The Radiation of the Liturgy into Catholic Homes*. Collegeville, MN: The Order of St. Benedict, Inc., 1956; Rockford, IL: TAN Books and Publishers, Inc., 1998.

978-0-595-50978-2
0-595-50978-9

Printed in the United States
122063LV00004B/21/P